"In this readable and insightful book, Dwight DuBois encourages us to put aside the sharp dichotomy between laity and clergy and our obsession with the church as organization and institution, and examine our vocation as a people at once gathered around Word and Sacrament and scattered into the world, the location of our calling and mission. He invites us to see the church at work in the world through its members who are "scattered" among the institutions, workplaces, and communities around us, and he envisions a diaconal church that is willing to risk losing its corporate life for the sake of the world God loves. Dwight DuBois has written an insightful and helpful gem of a book that will help the church understand its vocation and its mission in our current challenging context."

—H. JULIAN GORDY
Bishop, ELCA Southeastern Synod

THE SCATTERING

Deborah,

 May God continue
to work for the ~~Ca~~
Dream in all the
ministries of your
life.   Dwight W Ro

THE SCATTERING

Imagining a Church that Connects Faith and Life

Dwight L. DuBois

Foreword by Craig L. Nessan

with an Interlude by Forrest Walden

WIPF & STOCK · Eugene, Oregon

THE SCATTERING
Imagining a Church that Connects Faith and Life

Wipf & Stock
An Imprint of Wipf and Stock Publishers
199 W. 8th Ave., Suite 3
Eugene, OR 97401

www.wipfandstock.com

ISBN 13: 978-1-4982-2978-4

Manufactured in the U.S.A.   12/17/2015

The gifts he gave were that some would be apostles, some prophets, some evangelists, some pastors and teachers, to equip the saints for the work of ministry, for building up the body of Christ, until all of us come to the unity of the faith and of the knowledge of the Son of God, to maturity, to the measure of the full stature of Christ.

EPHESIANS 4:11–13

Contents

Foreword

"Imagination is more important than knowledge" (Albert Einstein). The Reformation fostered amazing imagination for the renewal of the church through the reinvigoration of the universal priesthood. Luther and the Reformers imagined a church in which all members of the church were so grounded in their baptismal identity in Jesus Christ that they would claim their Christian vocation to live out this calling in all the occupations of daily life. This imagination was to serve as a corrective to a hierarchical structure, in which clerics climbed the ranks of power and privilege, effectively defining and controlling what it meant to be church. For many historical reasons what unfolded after the Reformation were instead new forms of clericalism, according to which evolved ever new dependency structures of the laity upon the clergy. While there have been exceptions to this pattern, for example among the churches of the Radical Reformation, the exceptions prove the rule among the Protestant mainstream.

Dwight DuBois here kindles again as for the first time imagination for a church that discovers its vitality and purpose through the sending of members into all the nooks and crannies of their varied lives. The language used is original and dynamic: the gathered church must always be seen in dynamic relationship to what he provocatively names the scattered church. This means that the mission of the gathered church always entails the formation of the baptized for connecting faith and life. Even more, it means holding all the baptized, clergy and laity, accountable for asking how their daily ministries have led to the service of neighbors in the world as often as the church regathers. This language has promise for moving us beyond clergy/lay dichotomies, insofar as all members are to be fully engaged in neighbor love as the aim of the Gospel's mission. This vision and language provide a fresh way of interpreting who we are and what we do as the church of Jesus Christ.

The author's proposal is based on an intuition about the need for the revival of the institutional church based on that holy imagination, as it originated in the Holy Scriptures and bubbled up again at the time of the Reformation. This book, however, offers much more than intuition, or even imagination. This book provides fascinating qualitative research about an inexplicable gap between pastors and church members regarding their perceptions of whether and how the church is succeeding "to equip the saints for the work, building up the body of Christ" (Eph 4:12). The disparity between the responses of pastors and church members related to this line of inquiry is nothing short of stunning. DuBois carefully analyzes and interprets where the problem lies, aptly naming the resistance to change as the church's "autoimmune disorder." An autoimmune disorder involves the body's immune system errantly attacking and destroying healthy body tissue. If the church is the body of Christ, our autoimmune disorder involves the subtle yet manifold ways that the church establishes institutional survival as its real agenda at the expense of connecting the following of Jesus with serving everyday neighbors—at home or school, in the workplace and community, locally and globally. While DuBois clearly affirms the critical importance of the gathered church, including a robust infrastructure, the fundamental alignment of the church's business always needs to be oriented toward sending people out of the church's doors, rather than capturing them inside a building.

As the author articulates, vital church communities always are in motion between those things that are essential to forming identity in Christ Jesus and those things that proceed outwards in mission based on that identity. The church's autoimmune disorder interrupts the God-intended ceaseless cycle between the gathering and the sending. Mending the church's theology of ordained ministry is key to healing this disorder. Only when the pastors of Christ's church understand ordination itself as ultimately in service to the ministry of the baptized in the world can our stuck church system begin to be reformed. How can the ministry of Word and sacrament be reimagined and reoriented? We must understand that the proclamation of the Word and administration of the sacraments are finally, according to Luther, about Christian freedom. This means the proclamation of the Gospel and the sacramental encounter with Jesus Christ are about *freedom from* everything that impedes us from being and living as the persons God created us to be. And the means of grace always also equally involve *freedom for* loving and serving the neighbors, whom God gives us every moment of our lives! Bonhoeffer's warning about the dangers of "cheap grace" continues to hit us in the gut. We bask in our "freedom from" sin, death, and the devil. But we continue to suffer from our chronic autoimmune disorder in relation to "freedom for" serving neighbors in our families, daily work, local communities, and global relationships. The ongoing reformation of the church is inextricably dependent upon the conversion of pastors to recognize and affirm that ordained ministry is to be directed entirely toward the vitality of a servant church lived out in the everyday lives of church members.

A renewed appreciation for the ancient office of the deacon has potential to serve as another catalyst for the New Reformation imagined in this book. The ministry of Jesus Christ was itself in essence diaconal ministry, the ministry of service to neighbors in need. Deacons exist for the sake of connecting church and world, bringing the needs of the world to the attention of the church and the compassion of Christ through the church in ministering to those needs. While deacons function as those who themselves are engaged in addressing the world's gaping needs through direct service, even more crucial for the future of the church is the role of the deacon in *catalyzing the ministry of the laity* as agents of Christ's mission in all the arenas of their daily lives. If ministers of Word and sacrament are able to catch the vision of a diaconal church, then they can become the greatest allies and boosters of the ministry of deacons, learning to work in partnership with deacons for the sake of the ministry of the baptized as the ultimate *telos* of God's purposes for the church. "Then comes the end, when Jesus Christ hands over the kingdom to God the Father, after he has destroyed every ruler and every authority and power" (1 Cor 15:24). The shalom of God, which Jesus described as the in-breaking of the kingdom, means that healing, reconciliation, forgiveness, and loving service belong to the future of God's purposes for the entire world. The church serves as an agent of God's shalom for the life of the world or is no body of Christ.

This book provides much practical grist for how the church may not only imagine but also implement practices for transforming the church from a status quo whose future bodes continuing decline into a servant church, "a caring church that longs to be a partner in Christ's sacrifice and clothed in Christ's humanity."[1] The Einstein quote cited above concludes: "For knowledge is limited to all we now know and understand, while

---

1. "The Church of Christ, in Every Age," by Fred Pratt Green. © 1971 Hope Publishing Company, Carol Stream, IL 60188. All rights reserved.

imagination embraces the entire world, and all there ever will be to know and understand." Because God in Christ by the power of the Spirit has not yet fulfilled the divine purposes of equipping a dynamic servant church through the full engagement of the baptized in Christian neighborliness, we have reason to continue to pray and hope and work for what the Triune God yet intends to accomplish among us, "so that God may be all in all" (1 Cor 15:28).

Craig L. Nessan, Academic Dean
Wartburg Theological Seminary, Dubuque, Iowa
Ordinary Time 2015

A Word of Thanks

This book is dedicated in thanksgiving to everyone who helped me along the way. I cannot let this opportunity pass without thanking my wife, Janice, for her support. She was a constant companion through much of the journey described in this book. She poked and prodded my thinking in appropriate and helpful ways. She graciously supported my desire to write this book.

I cannot begin to name all of the other individuals that were involved, as the list would include hundreds of people. Colleagues, members, and friends: you know who you are. You talked with me, shared your thoughts and insights, your questions and struggles. Many of you patiently listened while I wanted to talk about little else. Thank you. This book would not have been possible without you. May God continue to use you as, together, we equip the saints for the work of ministry, so that all people and all creation may experience God's love and care.

Introduction

Imagine a church that has a huge impact on society. Imagine a church that feeds the hungry in countless ways and places. Imagine a church that provides healing, comfort, and care for the sick and suffering—every day, near and far. Imagine a church with resources that total trillions of dollars. Imagine a church engaged in ministry that is so far-reaching that it's impossible to count, categorize, or report. That is the vision I have for the church.

Only this vision doesn't depend on leaders creating new initiatives, asking people to do something more, or raising more money. In fact, just the opposite may be true.

How is that possible? How can the church have far-reaching ministries without asking people to give more or do more? It's rather simple, actually: by acknowledging that the church—the people of God—is already engaged in feeding the hungry (parents and farmers do it every day), healing the sick (doctors, nurses, and pharmacists do this around the clock), working for common good (we do this when we vote or volunteer in community organizations), and engaging in countless other acts by which God is actively at work in us and through us for the welfare of the other—whoever, whatever, and wherever that may be.

This vision can be achieved by acknowledging the vast amount of ministry that is already taking place *outside the church*, by equipping people to do that work faith-fully, by commissioning all of us for our various ministries, by intentionally acknowledging and talking about how we are doing with our God-given callings, and by offering forgiveness and a chance to try again when we fail. In order to achieve this vision, we may actually need to cut back on our programs, our fundraisers, and our pleas for volunteers. We definitely need to stop seeing congregational ministries in competition with the daily lives and activities of Christ's followers. Not all ministry happens, or needs to happen, in and through the gathered church.

Hear this: what we do as the church gathered is important. Meeting regularly for worship is important. Forming faith in children and adults is important. Working together to fight hunger or eliminate malaria is important. In situations like these, we can do more together than we can separately. But hear this as well: what we do as the church scattered is equally important. It's not an either/or choice; it is most definitely a matter of being church and joining God's mission when we're gathered *and* when we're scattered.

The principal reason we have not achieved this vision is because we have been preoccupied with the health and viability of the church-as-institution for far too long. In our dedication to maintaining this model of *church* we have overlooked, and sometimes even denigrated, wonderful and encouraging acts of ministry that happen every day—*in the world.*

My premise is this: *When we become as good at the scattering of the church as we are at its gathering, we will find new joy, new purpose, and new vitality.* We will embody the biblical calling of the church as those who are blessed by God to bless others. We will take pressure off both leaders and members who fear the decline of the congregation's vitality and relevance. We will be amazed to realize how far and wide God is at work in us and through us for the sake of our neighbor.

A JOURNEY OF DISCOVERY AND RENEWED HOPE

This book is a story about a journey. It's the story of the church's corporate journey over the past decades and even centuries, and it's the story of my own personal journey in recent years. It's the story of how dedicated seminary professors labored to form me—and pastors like me—so that I would be aware of and supportive of the ministry that all the baptized have in daily life. It's also the story of how I—and pastors like me, caught up in the demands of parish life—lost that vision. It's the story of surprising discoveries, and the story of how some of those discoveries were wrong. It's the story of how many individuals and groups have labored year after year to restore the vision of a church that supports and empowers the priesthood of all believers, only to see that vision set aside because we could not make a direct connection between the vitality of the institution and all that we do in God's name in our everyday lives.

This book is based in hope. It's a hope that one of the fundamental precepts of the church—that the church exists not for itself but for the sake of the world—can restore a sense of purpose, vitality, and even joy to the faithful remnant that is reeling from decades of loss: loss of purpose, loss of relevance, and loss of members. It's a hope that we can recast the role of the church in terms of supporting all believers for their ministry in the world, and thereby relieve the stress that comes with a narrow focus on keeping programs humming and finances healthy.

This book is also based on the hope—the promise even—that by re-forming our congregations as communities that prepare, support, encourage, equip, and send people into the world as God's partners in the care and restoration of all creation, leaders in congregations—pastors in particular—will find new meaning, new vitality, new purpose, and even joy in their various ministries. Living out the vision of ministry as something that is shared by *all* God's people rather than provided to God's people by a chosen few holds the promise of lifting heavy burdens from threadbare shoulders.

In this regard, a word of caution is in order: As you read this book you may find yourself burdened by thoughts, approaches, suggestions, changes, or activities that appear to be additional demands. I can only encourage you to hold onto the premise and the promise that this book is more about letting go than it is about adding on. By letting go of our preoccupation with congregational programs, in finding ways to measure vitality in terms other than contributions and attendance, and by seeing ministry as something that has been given to all God's people, my hope is that we will find new ways to celebrate all that God is doing and wants to do in the world through *all* of us, both in the church and in the world.

A ROSE BY ANY OTHER NAME

The subject of this book has gone by many names over the years: priesthood of all believers, ministry of the laity, vocation, ministry in daily life, calling, purpose, and most recently I've seen it called "spirituality in the workplace." Even though it has been known by a wide variety of names, and maybe precisely *because* it has been known by many names, there is no dominant way to describe it. Every time a name has been popularized, it has been sidetracked or diminished, either by resistance, by confused interpretations, or (to use a phrase that describes the unintentional expansion of an endeavor beyond its original goals) by the inevitable "mission creep" that infects all such movements. Personally, I like *vocation*, but that word is difficult to use because many people see it only in terms of a job (hence vocational schools where students are taught skills to perform a particular job), while others see it only in terms of a call to religious service (the priesthood or the convent in particular). Sometimes the word is so foreign to listeners that they think the speaker simply mispronounced *vacation*. Over the course of this journey I used *ministry in daily life* because it was the best option I had, but even that phrase has its drawbacks. In this book I use alternative language based on gathering and scattering that holds the potential to move us forward, though at times I revert to older language as well. My reading of Scripture and my understanding of what happens in the waters of baptism convince me that God's intent is that all of us are called to be God's agents of love, reconciliation, hope, and service. That call certainly applies to what we do when we gather as church, but it applies equally (and perhaps even more so) in the scattering—in the roles, relationships, and responsibilities of our everyday lives.

WHO SHOULD READ THIS BOOK

This book is principally for people who are or will be leaders in local congregations: those who are financially compensated for their leadership, those who are training for paid or unpaid roles in the church, those who are elected or appointed to leadership roles, and volunteers serving as informal leaders in small groups or other relational roles. Even if you are not a leader in your congregation, if you are searching for a way to renew and revitalize both your faith and the faith journey of your congregation, you may find hope and purpose in these pages.

A word of confession: I am a Lutheran pastor, and so (for better or worse) I am most familiar with Lutheran viewpoints, history, theology, and language, and I am most familiar with leadership from the pastor's point of view. Nevertheless, I worked to keep this book as accessible as possible to readers from many denominations, with varying degrees of theological education, and different ministry credentials. Even so, it needs to be noted that some readers will encounter new words or foreign languages. Please know that I don't do this to intimidate or discourage anyone. It's just that in some cases these words, when they are carefully explored and explained, can bring new insight to old expectations and understandings.

In order to broaden the base upon which this book is written, I interviewed people from a wide variety of mainline denominations. This means the findings presented here are applicable across denominational lines. While I often speak Lutheranese and quote Martin Luther more than you might be accustomed to, I also include insights from other traditions. Regardless of your background, I hope you will find insight and new hope for the ministry of the church in these pages.

LOOKING AHEAD

Some of what you find in this book is not new with me. This is due, in part, to the long history the church has had with this topic (which you will hear more about in chapter 4). In addition, some of what I present here is available in other places, but you would have to spend months reading a wide variety of books in order to find it on your own. The good news for me is that I have not had to reinvent the wheel; in places I either summarize or quote the work of others. The good news for you is that if you want more information on any particular point, you can find many sources in the footnotes and read to your heart's content.

What *is* new here falls into three categories:

1) my personal journey of rediscovering this call to service in the world—a journey that I am confident is shared by many people in the church;

2) the results of interviewing and observing many congregational leaders and members about the confusion that inhibits progress in this area; and

3) new language that overcomes stereotypes and opens the door to new ways of being and doing church.

The first two chapters set the stage. We will not make any progress toward equipping and sending the saints if we do not first understand the nature and purpose of the church. Chapter 1 covers that ground, then provides some initial language for this journey. Chapter 2 looks at the conversations I had with pastors and their people that I referred to in point 2) above. Chapters 3 and 4 are foundational for those who want to explore the biblical and theological grounding of the call to ministry that God gives to all believers. Chapter 3 looks at the perceived difference between clergy and laity, and then points to a way that we can talk about ministry in terms of our common calling. Chapter 4 follows up with a review of vocation from biblical times, through the Reformation, and into our day. We find that the gathered church has consistently overlooked the church's essential task of equipping the saints for ministry.

Chapter 5 then serves as a turning point from what has been to what might be. It proposes an alternate way of describing the life and ministry of the gathered and scattered church. Following that, chapters 6 and 7 describe essential characteristics for a church that connects faith and life. Chapter 6 looks at the road ahead in terms of dying to our corporate selves so that we are free to love and serve our neighbors. Chapter 7 builds some framework that will enable us to become communities that equip the saints. The final chapter is a foretaste of practical ways by which congregational leaders can begin to implement the premise of this book. I hope these initial ideas will inspire real-world experimentation in your setting. Who knows what might happen? With a little help from the Holy Spirit, a new way of being and doing church is ready to leap from your imagination into life-giving practice. When that happens, I hope you will share your experiments and your experiences at www.TheScattering.org, the companion website for this book. Together we can create and share resources that can help the church live into the promise of the priesthood of all believers.

Abbreviations

BCP   *Book of Common Prayer*

ELW   *Evangelical Lutheran Worship*

LW   *Luther's Works* (in English)

OED   *Oxford English Dictionary*

UMH   *The United Methodist Hymnal*

WA   *Luther's Works* (the Weimar Edition, in German)

1

Imagining a New/old Church
—Gathered and Sent

Think of how the word *church* is used. "I'm going to church tomorrow," means of course, I'm planning to go to worship tomorrow. "My church believes in the Bible" could be a reference to the theological orientation of a congregation or of a denomination. "Our church is open to all people" might mean the congregation is intentionally inclusive, or it might mean that community groups can meet in the building. Or someone might ask, "Where is your church?" when they want to know the location of the building. While the easy answer is "We're located a block from the high school," I've heard a few people respond to this question by saying, "Well, let's see: It's Thursday afternoon so Sue is at her office at the insurance company, Bob is probably driving to his next site visit, and Billy is headed home from school." Of course, this last answer would only confuse people who just want to know the location of the building. These common uses of *church* are so prevalent that few Christians even question them.

While *church* is often equated with a building, denomination, congregation, or a worship service, these things are not *church* in its fullest, richest sense. Because of that, we begin our pursuit of what it means to equip the saints for the work of ministry (Eph 4:12) by first seeking to understand the nature and purpose of the church. This isn't just an academic exercise; such theological and practical grounding is necessary in order to know who we are and what God is calling us to be and do, both as a community of believers and as individuals. This chapter traces the purpose of God's

1

people through the Old Testament, into the New, and then over the history of the church. We will wind up with some new (well, actually, it's quite old) language that will help us grow into all that God desires us to be.

SHALOM

Any understanding of the church needs to start with an understanding of God's desire for the world. So let's start at the beginning: "God saw everything that he had made, and indeed, it was very good" (Gen 1:31). A better translation would be, "God saw everything that had been created, and indeed, it was exactly what God had in mind." Creation was the way God wanted it to be; all creation and all creatures were in harmony. It was paradise. It was a wonderful and life-giving place to be.

The word in the Hebrew language for this condition is *shalom*. Despite it being a Hebrew word, it is well known around the world; most people translate it as "peace." It means that, but it includes much more. Like the Hawaiian word *Aloha*, *shalom* is used both to greet people and to bid them farewell. But wait! There's more! Shalom means completeness, soundness, welfare, peace, safety, prosperity, quiet, tranquility, contentment, and friendship. It is also used to describe peace with God, especially in the context of a covenant with God. One English word that is missing from this list is a helpful way to sum up many of the synonyms: *harmony*.

This long list of words that translate *shalom* is a great place to begin our look at God's desire for the world. Words like completeness, peace, prosperity, and harmony describe the way God intended life to be from the very beginning; they describe that which God desires for us, for all people, and for all creation.

But it doesn't take long before Genesis describes what happened to this vision of shalom. By the time we get to the third chapter, sin enters in, and God's beautiful vision is broken. The story of Adam and Eve and how they messed up creation is not an irrelevant old tale. It is also our story. This is the story of how our lack of trust in God's goodness causes us to take our God-given freedom, responsibility, and relationships and abuse them, rendering us broken images of God, broken reminders of God's presence and care in the world.

As tragic as the story is, it is important to note that brokenness is not the last word. In a verse that is easily overlooked, God's grace and continuing concern for the well-being of creation is shown. Genesis 3:21 says,

"And the Lord God made garments of skins for the man and for his wife, and clothed them." God knew that clothes made of fig leaves would not protect Adam and Eve from the harshness of life outside the garden. So even after pronouncing judgment on them, and before driving them out of the garden, God made decent clothes that would protect them. This was an act of pure and undeserved grace; God continues to care for both creature and creation.

By the sixth chapter of Genesis, humanity had plumbed the depths of decadence. Verses 5 and 6 read, "The Lord saw that the wickedness of humankind was great in the earth, and that every inclination of the thoughts of their hearts was only evil continually. And the Lord was sorry that he had made humankind on the earth, and it grieved him to his heart." God's judgment on human beings, though, did not bring God to a total destruction of all life. Rather, God chose Noah who, according to 6:8, had "found favor in the sight of the Lord." Noah and his family were told that, through them, God would make a fresh beginning.

The story of Noah and the ark is followed immediately by the story of the tower of Babel, where we see people in their false sense of pride trying build a tower high enough to reach God. Chapter 12 of Genesis tells of an important turning point in God's relationship to humanity. Here God's covenant with Abraham is introduced: "The Lord said to Abram, 'Go from your country and your kindred and your father's house to the land that I will show you. I will make of you a great nation, and I will bless you, and make your name great, so that you will be a blessing . . . in you all the families of the earth shall be blessed' " (12:1–3). God's *promise* was that Abram's descendants would become a mighty nation; the *reason* for this promise was to make God's love known to all people. Through the rest of the Old Testament we find the record of this nation's life; we read of their triumphs and their tragedies. As the eons passed, the people remained stubborn and resistant, but God kept trying. Prophets, priests, kings all labored to bring back shalom, always with the same disappointing result.

God's attempts to fix the brokenness of creation, to restore shalom, is one of the strongest themes in the Old Testament. Like Adam and Eve and all their descendants, we too deserve God's judgment. But Scripture tells the ongoing story of God who never gave up on us. God never said in desperation, "I'll let my people fend for themselves, if that's what they want so desperately!" Instead, through the centuries God continually sought to fix this broken creation, or to use a Genesis 3:21 metaphor, to clothe us

3

in righteousness. Despite our brokenness, God continually pursues us in love, seeking to restore us to the position we were intended to occupy in creation from the beginning—as God's chosen representatives and partners on earth, that everyone and everything might live in shalom.

The stories of God's attempts to fix the brokenness of creation sound like a tennis match: God keeps hitting the ball into our court, trying to score the winning point, but we keep slamming it back across the net, saying, "Try again!" It must have been a terribly frustrating process, but as we know, God keeps on trying. This saga is summed up in the New Testament's parable of the wicked tenants:

> [Jesus] began to speak to them in parables. "A man planted a vineyard, put a fence around it, dug a pit for the wine press, and built a watchtower; then he leased it to tenants and went to another country. When the season came, he sent a slave to the tenants to collect from them his share of the produce of the vineyard. But they seized him, and beat him, and sent him away empty-handed. And again he sent another slave to them; this one they beat over the head and insulted. Then he sent another, and that one they killed. And so it was with many others; some they beat, and others they killed. He had still one other, a beloved son. Finally he sent him to them, saying, 'They will respect my son.' " (Mark 12:1–6)

We know how this story played out. We met God's ultimate volley, drove Jesus back across the eternal net, and thought that we had run God off the court once and for all. But the story doesn't end with our response; it doesn't end with the crucifixion. In a sermon on the incarnation of Jesus, Clarence Jordan describes the resurrection in these terms:

> By raising Jesus from the dead, God is refusing to take man's "No" for an answer. He's saying, "You can kill my boy if you wish, but I'm going to raise him from the dead, and put him right smack dab down there on earth again!" It's God saying, "I'm not going to take man's 'No' for an answer. I'm going to raise him up, plant his feet on the earth, and put him to preaching, teaching and healing again."[1]

And God's means for planting Jesus' feet on the earth, God's means for continuing the preaching, teaching and healing, was through none other than a chosen and called-out people—commonly known as the church. We are God's hands, healing the brokenness of the world. We are God's mouth,

---

1. Jordan, *Substance of Faith*, 28.

speaking words of restoration and hope. We are God's body, broken-yet-restored people living together as a demonstration and an instrument of shalom: completeness, peace, prosperity, perfectness, and harmony.

THE KINGDOM (DREAM) OF GOD

As we just saw, it's not hard to explain the Hebrew notion of shalom. With a little work, we can take the concept from the familiar notion of peace to a fuller, richer understanding.

Interestingly, though, when Jesus arrives on the scene he doesn't talk about shalom. He proclaims and demonstrates a way of life that is identical to shalom, but he uses a phrase that takes a good bit of work to translate for a contemporary audience: the kingdom of God (or its twin, the kingdom of heaven).

When North Americans today read the New Testament, we're often tripped up by this imagery. We don't live under a monarchy, so *kingdom of God* can leave us confused. For a lack of a better explanation, people often define the kingdom of God (or the kingdom of heaven) as that place you go after you die or as a paradise that begins after this world ends. Sometimes that kingdom is nothing more than an inner feeling of peace and contentment, a Christian form of nirvana.

Scholars have attempted other metaphors to get at the heart of Jesus' proclamation. Sometimes the word *reign of God* is used.[2] Jesus demonstrated and proclaimed a new reign that was wholly different from the political reign of Rome. In this new reign insiders would be outsiders, and the bottom would become the top. In that light, *reign* has some advantages, but it, too, can be problematic. Craig Nessan has experimented with several metaphors; one of the most intriguing is "the dream of God."[3] If we use "the dream of God" in every place that Jesus mentions "the kingdom of God" or "the kingdom of heaven," then we have a better chance of understanding what Jesus was proclaiming and demonstrating: Jesus was working to restore nothing less than God's dream of shalom.

Read this description of shalom, and see if it doesn't sound a lot like Jesus' proclamation of the kingdom of God:

---

2. Cox, *Future of Faith*, 45. Cox prefers to use "the reign*ing* of God" to imply "something that is going on—not a place, but a 'happening.'"

3. Nessan, *Beyond Maintenance*, 30.

Shalom involves all members of God's creation living in harmonious and life-giving relationship with one another. Shalom begins with the prayerful and worshipful relationship of the human being with God. . . . Shalom at the same time entails human beings living together in harmony with each other, both sharing what is needed for the physical well-being of all and nurturing one another emotionally and spiritually. . . . Furthermore . . . shalom involves human beings living in balance with and respect for the whole of creation.[4]

The central theme of Jesus' proclamation was this: God's resurrected dream of shalom has come near. He sent out the disciples, "As you go, proclaim the good news, 'The kingdom of heaven has come near.'" (Matt 10:7) And what is that good news? What does that kingdom/reign/dream look like?

When [Jesus] came to Nazareth, where he had been brought up, he went to the synagogue on the sabbath day, as was his custom. He stood up to read, and the scroll of the prophet Isaiah was given to him. He unrolled the scroll and found the place where it was written:
"The Spirit of the Lord is upon me,
        because he has anointed me
                to bring good news to the poor.
He has sent me to proclaim release to the captives
        and recovery of sight to the blind,
                to let the oppressed go free,
        to proclaim the year of the Lord's favor."
And he rolled up the scroll, gave it back to the attendant, and sat down. The eyes of all in the synagogue were fixed on him. Then he began to say to them, "Today this scripture has been fulfilled in your hearing." (Luke 4:16–21)

Or try this view:

Then I saw a new heaven and a new earth; for the first heaven and the first earth had passed away, and the sea was no more. And I saw the holy city, the new Jerusalem, coming down out of heaven from God, prepared as a bride adorned for her husband. And I heard a loud voice from the throne saying,
        "See, the home of God is among mortals.
        He will dwell with them as their God;

---

4. Nessan, *Shalom Church*, 10.

they will be his peoples,
and God himself will be with them;
he will wipe every tear from their eyes.
Death will be no more;
mourning and crying and pain will be no more,
for the first things have passed away." (Rev 21:1–4)

The message of the New Testament is clear: Jesus introduces, demonstrates, and proclaims a new way of life. Actually, it's a very old way of life, one that had its start in the Garden of Eden. Jesus intended that this dawning reality would reshape the course of human events by reintroducing the concept of shalom.[5]

> Jesus taught and enacted the coming of God's peaceable and just kingdom in his parables, teachings, and ministry. . . . The coming of the kingdom meant spiritual reunion between God and humankind through the forgiveness of sins and reconciling love. At the same time the emergence of God's kingdom entailed the healing of disease, the exorcism of demons, miraculous feeding of the hungry, restoration of broken relationships, and the promise of a bounteous creation.[6]

Far from being a kingdom that can be found only in the afterlife, the dream of God is near; it is something that is happening here and now, in this world. In giving this ministry to the disciples after his resurrection, Jesus passed it on to us, the church. Like Jesus, the church's purpose is to introduce, demonstrate, and proclaim the nearness of God's dream—not just for our benefit, but for the sake of all people and all creation.

WELL-INTENTIONED REDEFINITION FELL SHORT

It's not possible to look at the purpose of the church without considering understandings that we have inherited over the centuries. If you ask Lutheran pastors about the definition of the church, they will point to Article VII of the Augsburg Confession: "It is also taught among us that one holy Christian church will be and remain forever. This is the assembly of all believers among whom the Gospel is preached in its purity and the holy sacraments are administered according to the Gospel."[7] The Gospel preached

---

5. See Van Gelder, *Essence of the Church*, 76.

6. Nessan, *Shalom Church*, 10–11.

7. Kolb and Tappert, *Book of Concord*, 42.

in its purity and the sacraments rightly administered continue to be two of the bedrock principles of the Lutheran church. Similarly, in the Institutes of Christian Religion, John Calvin notes, "the marks by which the Church is to be distinguished, are, the preaching of the word, and the administration of the sacraments."[8] A few years after the Augsburg Confession, the Belgic Confession of 1561 (the doctrinal standard for many Reformed traditions) added a third criterion, the exercise of church discipline. In response to the reformers, Catholic theologians of the time countered with their own definition of the church in the Council of Trent. They said that the church "consists in its unity," and that unity is shown in its one invisible ruler, Christ, and one visible ruler, the Pope.[9]

These definitions may have been appropriate and helpful in their day, but over time they have led to less than healthy understandings. The Catholic Church judged its purity by its authority and leadership. Protestants became preoccupied with doctrinal purity, not only over against the Catholic Church but in struggles between various brands of Protestantism.

In recent years the Catholic definition has shifted from authority and leadership to a gathered community. The Catechism of the Catholic Church says:

> In Christian usage, the word "church" designates the liturgical assembly, but also the local community or the whole universal community of believers. These three meanings are inseparable. "The Church" is the People that God gathers in the whole world. She exists in local communities and is made real as a liturgical, above all a Eucharistic, assembly. She draws her life from the word and the Body of Christ and so herself becomes Christ's Body.[10]

---

8. Calvin, *Institutes*, 4.1.10. Calvin *does* describe the church as the people elsewhere in Book IV. In chapter 2 he maintains that the Nicene Creed "refers not only to the visible Church . . . but likewise to all the elect of God, including the dead as well as the living." In chapter 7 he notes that *church* is used in two senses. Sometimes Scripture refers to it as "that [institution or organism] which is really such in the sight of God, into which none are received but those who by adoption and grace are the children of God." But, he notes, *church* is also used "to designate the whole multitude dispersed all over the world, who profess to worship one God and Jesus Christ." In chapters 9 and 10, though, when talking about the former, he uses language very much like the Augsburg Confession: "For wherever we find the word of God purely preached and heard, and the sacraments administered according to the institution of Christ, there, it is not to be doubted, is a Church of God."

9. Bosch, *Transforming Mission*, 248.

10. *Catholic Catechism.* See Part One, "The Profession of Faith;" Section Two, "The Profession of the Christian Faith;" Chapter Three, "I Believe in the Holy Spirit;" Article

For the purposes of this discussion that is a more helpful definition. It is clear about the nature of the church as gathered community, but one would be hard pressed to identify the role of the church in the world in this definition. Likewise, Protestant scholars have argued for an understanding of the church that goes beyond it being a "place where certain things happen."[11] We are inheritors of definitions that were created hundreds of years ago in response to serious challenges within and among the churches, yet we have a hard time moving beyond these definitions of church-as-place or church-as-vendors of religious goods and services.

MISSIO DEI AND MISSIONAL CONGREGATIONS

In the late 1990s, I returned to seminary for an advanced degree in missiology (the study of the mission of the church). I did this at the peak of the conversation about *missional church,* an effort to redefine the nature and purpose of the church for our time. The missional church movement was an attempt to redefine the nature of the church so that churches might go out and engage the world, rather than merely offer programs and activities designed to draw people in. Based on the concept of *missio Dei* (the mission of God), scholars sought to tie God's missionary nature to the sending of the church: "The classical doctrine of the *missio Dei* as God the Father sending the Son, and God the Father and the Son sending the Spirit [is] expanded to include yet another 'movement': Father, Son, and Holy Spirit sending the church into the world."[12]

Based on texts like John 20:21, "As the Father has sent me, so I send you," the movement sought to inspire a new era of congregations that were focused on mission, not just as an optional program of the church, but as a definition of the church's nature. "We have learned to speak of God as a 'missionary God.' Thus we have learned to understand the church as a 'sent people.'"[13] It is also important to note that the scholars were not pushing

9, "I Believe in the Holy Catholic Church;" Paragraph 1, "The Church in God's Plan." The Catechism is available in the public domain.

11. For additional insight into the definition of the church, see Hunsberger, *Between Gospel and Culture,* 337–342, where he compares the "church as place," the "church as vendor of religious goods and services" and the "church as a body of people sent on a mission."

12. Bosch, *Transforming Mission,* 390.

13. Guder, *Missional Church,* 4.

for mission in terms of something that happens overseas, but as something that happens outside the doors of our congregations and our homes.

As I transitioned out of that year of extended study, I had a newfound excitement to reenter parish ministry and apply what I had learned. As I started in my next call, I became acutely aware of the inwardness of the congregation I had been called to serve, so much of my work was dedicated to turning the focus outward. While it was (and continues to be) a healthy congregation with a rich music program, the congregation was less able to articulate its purpose in terms of making an impact in the world. Early in my tenure, I searched the Bible for references to the congregation's name and adapted Psalm 50:2 as a tagline for our collective work: "Out of Zion, God shines forth." Certainly God's presence shone in the internal activities of the congregation, but I wanted to lift up the reality that God wants to be known outside of the congregation as well.

Toward the end of my time at this congregation, we developed a mission statement to build on the tagline and to communicate our purpose: *Gathered to Grow, Sent to Shine.* While we (of course) thought it was brilliant, we realized that it was a bit cryptic, so we developed a flier that would put some meat on the bones. The experience of developing the flier reminds me of a story about my daughter.

Just before we moved from South Carolina to Iowa, my daughter was in the sixth grade, and since it was hurricane season she had been asked to write a report on hurricane preparedness. Knowing that we were about to move to Iowa, my daughter asked the teacher if she could also do a similar report on tornados. "Sure," the teacher said. My daughter's report on hurricane preparations went speedily: buy water, batteries, and canned foods; board up windows; store all loose items. It was easy to write a report since a list of tasks and supplies was printed on grocery store bags each fall. Having finished the first half of her report, my daughter asked, "Okay, Daddy, what do you do to prepare for a tornado?"

The experience of developing our flier was much the same. The first part, "Gathered to Grow," was simple. Examples of programs and activities flowed easily: attend or teach classes, participate in or lead worship, host or attend small groups, pray together or alone. In fact, it was hard to keep the list concise. With my daughter's second report, there wasn't much more to write than "Seek cover!" It was the same for the second half of our flier, "Sent to Shine." We included a couple generic sentences about ministry in daily life, but we were unable to come up with examples to illustrate it.

Throughout this period, from my time back at seminary through the years at this congregation, I had a nagging question rattling around in my subconscious. It was a question that wouldn't find conscious expression until I started working on the project that led to this book: *How can the church be missional?* If, when we hear *church,* we inherently think *congregation,* how is a congregation missional? Certainly we can send people on mission trips, we can sign people up to serve at the community shelter, we can enter a float in the Fourth of July parade, and our building can be highly visible at a busy intersection, but how, exactly, is a *congregation* missional?

As I look back on the books I read about the missional church, I see that the authors consistently use corporate language. Consider this exhortation:

> The church . . . is a people of God who are created by the Spirit
> to live as a missionary community. As such, the church is both a
> social organization and a spiritual community. . . . The church is
> God's personal presence in the world through the Spirit.[14]

The authors of *Missional Church* say, "The church as an alternative community can make a powerful witness when it chooses to live differently from the dominant society even at just a few key points."[15] "The church is a city on a hill."[16] "The missional church will be in the world with good news."[17] "The church is not simply a gathering of well-meaning individuals who have entered into a social contract to meet their privately defined self-interests. It is, instead, an intentional and disciplined community witnessing to the power and the presence of God's reign."[18] While these are all desirable outcomes, ultimately they are difficult things to give expression to corporately.

We should not be surprised then, that the authors rarely explain in concrete terms how that kind of mission is accomplished. There *is* a section in the book on how the church should teach or form *individuals* so that they "can preach, teach, and heal in the name of Jesus and can share his sufferings and resurrection life."[19] But again, it's very much like the second

---

14. Van Gelder, *Essence of the Church,* 25.

15. Guder, *Missional Church,* 127.

16. Ibid., 128–9.

17. Ibid., 137.

18. Ibid., 159.

19. Ibid., 141.

half of the flier we tried to write: only generic descriptions are given with no examples to illustrate it.

A section on spiritual practices follows in *Missional Church*. In the discussion of the practice of reconciliation the authors say that it "is not an individual and private matter, but an ecclesial practice that fosters, shapes, and sustains missional communities. Such a practice is an antidote to the competitive, alienating individualism of North American culture."[20] This could have been a wonderful opportunity to talk about how members, having learned and lived this within the life of the congregation, can practice their faith in an alienating culture—but the authors don't go there.

I don't mean to be overly critical of the missional church authors on this point. They earnestly sought to turn the church outward. They were right in the sense that the mission field is no longer overseas, but outside the doors of every church and in every Christian's home and community. They were right in saying that God's mission is not intended to get more people involved in what churches are doing, but to get churches more involved in what God is doing—in and for the world. But like many of us, the missional church scholars focused almost exclusively on *church* in terms of what we do together. To be sure, we do important and meaningful things when we are together; what is largely missing is the equally important ministry of God's missional *people* at work in and for the world.[21]

BUNGEE JUMPING CHRISTIANS

According to the New Testament (as we will see in chapter 4) the Spirit literally calls the church (that is, the *people*) out of the world, into a community

---

20. Ibid., 166.

21. Note: like many other attempts to redefine the church in our day, "missional church" and "missional theology" have also suffered from mission creep. They are now two of the most used, misused, and overused phrases in the church today. When it began, missional theology was a new (some would say renewed) field of study that offered hope for a mission-driven church in a post-modern, post-Christendom world. In the first part of the twenty-first century numerous practitioners in the emerging church movement and in various evangelical denominations started using the term to describe any and every type of non-traditional effort, from new congregation starts to experiments in intentional Christian community to coffeehouse and bar ministries. Alan Roxburgh, a leading theologian in the area, is known to have said that the terminology went from obscurity to banality in a mere decade. Indeed, for many the word *missional* has become cliché, and many church leaders are inclined to dismiss it as nothing more than a passé fad. That is indeed unfortunate.

where we are cleansed, fed, and empowered. This called-out community is meant to be an example, a demonstration plot, a light on a hill; others are supposed to see how we live, relate, and serve, and see in us a glimpse of God's in-breaking kingdom (dream). But the purpose of the gathering is not simply to make us feel good about ourselves or to look good to others. The people are also sent back out into the world to do for others as God has done for us.

In the tradition in which I grew up, works righteousness is a very bad thing. Works righteousness is the label for the misunderstanding that what we do (our works) will make us righteous, upright, or loved by God. The church of Martin Luther's time taught that there was something we *could* do, something we *should* do, *have* to do in fact, to merit God's love. Say this prayer and get forgiveness. Become a monk or a priest and be more godly. Buy this indulgence and get a free pass from purgatory. Through his study of Scripture Martin Luther, himself a monk, came to a different conclusion regarding the central point of faith: We are forgiven by God's grace. Period. We cannot buy or earn God's favor. It is a gift.

Luther rightfully rebelled against religious "works," such as buying and selling indulgences, but in time the prohibition against works righteousness got applied to *all* works: you don't get a reward by serving at the shelter or brownie points by living morally. The trouble is that, for many, Luther's prohibition has morphed into something radically different: the rejection of works righteousness became an understanding that since there is nothing we can do to *earn* God's love, there is nothing that we have to do *in response* to God's love.

But Luther never meant to ban all works. What we often forget is that as vehemently as Luther opposed works righteousness, he was equally vehement in support of loving deeds—as long as they weren't done to earn God's love or with any expectation of a reward for ourselves.

> If you find yourself in a work by which you accomplish something good for God, or the holy, or yourself, but not for your neighbor alone, then you should know that that work is not a good work. For each one ought to live, speak, act, hear, suffer, and die in love and service for another, even for one's enemies, a husband for his wife and children, a wife for her husband, children for their parents, servants for their masters, masters for their servants, rulers for their subjects and subjects for their rulers, so that one's hand,

mouth, eye, foot, heart and desire is for others; these are Christian works, good in nature.[22]

Gustaf Wingren, commenting on Luther's understanding of the role of faith and vocation, says, "the Christian lives at once in relation with God and with his neighbor, in heaven and on earth. We cannot isolate man's relationship with God, speaking only of faith and overlooking man's relationship with his neighbor."[23] To shrink volumes to a couple of sentences, according to Luther, faith in God and acts of love are aimed at different purposes. *Faith* is directed toward heaven and *love* is directed toward one's neighbor. Both faith in God and the call to love one's neighbor constitute an organic unity.[24]

Based on this, I suggest that the proper metaphor for us is bungee jumping Christians. If you're willing to take this leap with me, Christians are a lot like bungee jumpers, somewhere between the bridge and the gorge (somewhere between heaven and earth), living life in-between, oscillating back and forth from faith to love.[25]

When Luther says that *faith moves life's center from earth to heaven*[26] we find one movement of bungee jumping Christians. We are called from the world to gather in community, to participate in worship, prayer, and Bible study. But, just like bungee jumpers, there is another force at work at the same time—even while we're moving toward God. Just as faith moves life's center from earth to heaven, *acts of love move life's center from heaven to earth*. Living in God's love pulls us, propels us out into the world, to love and serve our neighbor. Luther insisted that good works have a role in the life of a Christian: good works exist for the earth and one's neighbor, not for eternity and God. God does not need our good works, Luther said, but our neighbor does.[27] As bungee jumping Christians, we are called to both a

22. Wingren, *Luther on Vocation*, 120. This is Wingren's translation of the (as yet not published in English) *Adventspostille* of 1522 from the *Weimar Edition* 10 1, 2, 41.

23. Ibid., 54.

24. Ibid., 73–74.

25. In order for this bungee jumping metaphor to work, it would be better to think of it, not in up and down terms like an actual bungee jumper, but in back-and-forth, in-and-out terms. God calls us to worship, week after week, to find forgiveness, to hear God's Word for us, and to grow in faith. But even as we're moving toward God in faith, there is this other force tugging at us, calling, and propelling us into the world to love and serve our neighbor.

26. Wingren, *Luther on Vocation*, 235.

27. In this discussion of the different directions of faith and love, I am indebted to

life of faith (directed toward God) and a life of love (directed to the world), at the same time.

Dropping the metaphor, we can put it this way: what happens in our congregations is important. Proclamation of the Word and celebration of the sacraments are important. Forgiving sins and binding up the broken-hearted are important. Forming faith in children and adults is important. Providing pastoral care is important. But all of these things are also coupled with empowerment, purpose, and sending. In worship we are fed and renewed, prepared and equipped to go back out as God's people to love and serve the world.

> Christian beliefs and practices are intended to foster a way of life as disciples of Jesus Christ that in turn send us into God's world to imitate the forgiveness, mercy and love of God. . . . The church of the future will empower and release the baptized to witness and testify and serve and in all ways bear God's creative love for all the world.[28]

AN ENDLESS LOOP

There are many other ways to look at this inward and outward movement, but for now we'll consider just one more. In the book *Beyond Maintenance to Mission*, Craig Nessan looks at this movement by way of a figure eight or infinity loop.[29] In Nessan's model the figure eight revolves around two poles: identity and mission.

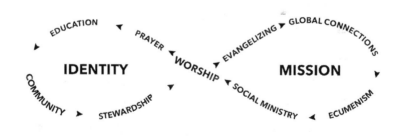

Wingren, *Luther on Vocation*, esp. pp. 10, 28, 54, 73 and 235, but throughout the book as well.

28. Frambach and Peterson "Church of the Future," 14–15.

29. Nessan, *Beyond Maintenance*, 9.

Neither focus may be omitted without distorting what I believe
to be the congregation's divine calling. Under the rubric of identity, we will consider the centrality of prayer, education, life in
community, and stewardship in forming a congregation's proper
self-understanding. Under the category of mission, attention
shifts to evangelizing, global connections, ecumenism, and social
ministry.[30]

Nessan is clear that the two foci are interrelated and each is necessary
for the other:

Focus on identity without mission reduces the church to a social
club whose only reason to exist is for the comfort and security
of its membership. Focus on mission without the nurture of baptismal identity—both personally and communally—begins to
disintegrate into hyperactivity without direction. Identity without
mission leads to self-absorption. Mission without identity leads
to amnesia and exhaustion. Both identity and mission must be
related in dynamic interaction.[31]

It is no small matter that Nessan places worship at the crossing point.
"The most important element for renewing congregational life involves reimagining what God is seeking to accomplish when the congregation gathers for worship."[32] Later on he adds, "*Worship is the single most important
factor in forming Christian identity.* Moreover, worship mediates the energy
that transforms congregations into centers for mission."[33]

GATHERED-SCATTERED PEOPLE

All of the above leads us to a critical part of our understanding of *church*:
When Jesus told Peter that he was a rock upon which he would build the
church (Matthew 16:18), he wasn't talking about a denomination or a
style of worship. When the author of the book of Revelation addressed the
seven churches of Asia Minor (chapters 2–4), he was not talking about the

---

30. Ibid., xii–xiii. Nessan notes on pg. 9 that this model might give the impression
that this is a linear process and that identity and mission are two different things, neither
of which is accurate. He proposes a more complex model to show their interdependency.
For our purposes, the infinity loop is sufficient; readers who want to explore the inter-
relatedness are urged to read the book.

31. Ibid., 7.

32. Ibid., xiii.

33. Ibid., 49. Emphasis in original.

buildings or the institution. In these and many other places, when the New Testament talks about the church it is referring to the people, people who trust in the risen Lord, Jesus Christ, who promises to love and forgive them.

Likewise, Luther defines the *church* as "the people" in his treatise, *On the Councils and the Church*:

> [S]etting aside various writings and analyses of the word "church," we shall this time confine ourselves simply to the Children's [Apostles'] Creed, which says, "I believe in one holy Christian church, the communion of saints." Here the creed clearly indicates what the church is, namely, a communion of saints, that is, a crowd or assembly of people who are Christians and holy, which is called a Christian holy assembly, or church. Yet this word "church" is not German and does not convey the sense or meaning that should be taken from this article [of the creed].[34]

Luther was not struggling with the English word *church*, but with the German *kirche* (kier'-ka). The etymology of the English word *church* is interesting; it can be traced back to a Middle English word that was based on the same root as the German word *kirche*. Both words were derived from the Greek word *kyriakos* (keer-ee-ah'-kos) that can be translated, "belonging to the Lord." *Church*, then, can be interpreted as "people who belong to the Lord." Considering the implications of baptism, when God claims us as God's own people, this word means much more than simply a building, an institution, or a worship service. Luther goes on in his treatise to bemoan the confusion caused by this word:

> If the words, "I believe that there is a holy Christian *people*," had been used in the Children's Creed, all the misery connected with this meaningless and obscure word ["church"] might easily have been avoided. For the words "Christian holy people" would have brought with them, clearly and powerfully, the proper understanding and judgment of what is, and what is not, church.[35]

In a more up-to-date version, Roger Swanson tells of preaching at a revival for the Lumbee Tribe of North Carolina. After the service, an elder of the church stayed behind to ask him, "Young man, do you know what the church is?" The elder's answer was, "What you have left over when the building burns down and the preacher leaves town."[36]

---

34. Luther, *LW* 41, 143.

35. Ibid., 41, 144, italics added.

36. Swanson, *Faith-Sharing Congregation*, 36.

Here then is the critical point in this understanding of *church*: in the New Testament, *the people are the church*. The people are church not only when we gather in one place (for instance, in worship); the people are also church when we scatter to live out our daily lives. The church is an expression of God's kingdom (dream) when we are gathered; in this state, as we move toward God in faith, we are a *sign* and *foretaste* of the kingdom (dream). The church is also an expression of God's kingdom (dream) when we are scattered; in this state, as we move toward our neighbor in love, we are *agents* and *instruments* of the kingdom.[37] Yet it's not quite that simple or clear cut: it's not that we are a sign and foretaste only when we are together, or agents and instruments only when we are scattered. Those are simply marks of our chief characteristics in those two states. We can and should be a sign and foretaste in our individual lives, and we can and should be agents and instruments of God's kingdom as a "collective person."[38]

The fact that we are, can, and should be the church scattered does not deny or diminish the purpose of or the need for us to be the church gathered. On the contrary, the experiences and the pressures of being the church scattered give purpose and meaning to the church gathered. Without the experience of being the church gathered, the church scattered will lose its power and purpose.

Likewise, the fact that we are, can, and should be the church gathered does not deny or diminish the purpose of or the need for the church scattered. Simply put, the church gathered dares not forget the fact that God's people are also called to be the church scattered; in fact, that is how most Christians spend most of their time. Indeed, the church gathered exists not for itself, but for the empowerment, encouraging, equipping, and sending of the church scattered.

Putting the last two paragraphs together, we can say that being the church gathered without making the move to being the church scattered leads to self-absorption. Being the church scattered without returning to the church gathered leads to amnesia and exhaustion.[39]

Commenting on Acts 1:8, "you will receive power when the Holy Spirit has come upon you; and you will be my witnesses in Jerusalem, in all Judea and Samaria, and to the ends of the earth," Chris Scharen says,

---

37. Guder, *Missional Church*, 101.

38. Nessan, *Shalom Church*, 42, 44–52. Nessan borrows and expands on this concept from Bonhoeffer.

39. See Nessan, *Beyond Maintenance*, 7, as quoted on p. 16, above.

> Here at the beginnings of the church we see the core impulse that
> has defined her life ever since. Gathered, we receive God's own self
> through holy word and holy food; scattered, we carry on Christ's
> work as his very body, upheld by his very Spirit, proclaiming his
> truth. . . . Who we are and are becoming in Christ is all for the sake
> of the world. We are gathered into Christ's body, the Church, for
> the work of scattering.[40]

NEW LANGUAGE FOR THE JOURNEY

I propose staking our understanding of *church* on the concept of our gath-
ered/scattered nature. Instead of talking about the institutional church or
the organization (with all of the baggage such terms carry), we can use
gathered church to describe this appropriate and necessary state of being
and doing. Instead of trying to force a square peg in a round hole with
any of the synonyms listed in the introduction (vocation, priesthood of all
believers, ministry in daily life), we can use *scattered church* to refer to this
appropriate and necessary expression of our life as God's people.

In fact, I will suggest later in the book that the distinction we often
make between clergy and laity can be overcome by talking about *gathered
ministers* and *scattered ministers*. At various times, we are ministers to and
among the people of God when we are the Body of Christ gathered. At other times and among other people we are ministers when we are the Body of
Christ scattered. (Beware of the tendency, though, to equate gathered ministers with the clergy or scattered church with the laity. As we will see later,
that belies the call to ministry that is given to all God's people in baptism.)

Likewise, by using a third variation of this language we can bridge the
gap between Sunday and the rest of the week. Instead of creating a false
dichotomy between what we do at church and what we do in the world,
talking about *gathered ministries* and *scattered ministries* will at once unify
the life of faith and help us speak more accurately about the various tasks
to which God calls us. By using this new (old) language, our congregations
will become more vital and relevant, the lay/clergy distinction will fade,
and the gap between Sunday and Monday will disappear.

But I get ahead of myself. The rest of this book will explore both the
language we are accustomed to using and this new way of speaking and
doing. In what follows, I will start using this language so that we might

---

40. Scharen, *Way of Life*, 111–2.

start imagining and acting our way into this new (old) way of being church. At times, though, particularly when speaking of the past, I will revert to former words and ways because this language was not available for the conversations and the research that paved the way for this book.

IN SUMMARY

To sum up what we've covered so far, from here on when I talk about *church* or the *Body of Christ* I mean the *people of God*, both as individuals and as a corporate reality, both the people scattered and the people gathered.

> It is the whole church that is the Body of Christ, the church at worship and the church at work, the church gathered and the church scattered. Christ's ministry continues through all the people, and not only when they are together in one place "in" what we call the church, but also when they are spread forth over the face of the earth living as disciples and ministers of Jesus Christ.[41]

Further, when I talk about *ministry* and *ministries* I mean care, comfort, service, support, encouragement, and other Christ-like acts. Gathered ministers and scattered ministers perform these acts, both when the church is gathered and when it is scattered.

Based on this foundation, then, we will consider what it means to cultivate an environment that is focused not on a congregation's vitality, but on sending the people of God into the world. But before we can do that we need to examine a bit of resistance that keeps cropping up, threatening to derail this vital work.

---

41. Crabtree, *Empowering Church*, 30.

2

A Gap in Imagination

A friend told me the story of encountering a woman who works at a Walgreens pharmacy.[1] The woman told a heart-warming story of her work and of her concern for what she saw as "her congregation," that is, the customers she had come to know and care for over time. In particular she talked about an uninsured mother who needed a $400 prescription for a child. "I worry and wonder," the woman behind the counter said. "What will this mother have to give up so that her child will have the medication he needs?"

My friend, a pastor who works on staff in a mid-level judicatory, commended the woman for her care and compassion, and then asked, "Does your church know that they have a minister working at Walgreens?"

"My church?" the woman asked with some surprise. "Why, no. I hadn't thought about that." She paused in confusion and then added, "They wouldn't think that this is important."

That story broke my heart. It saddened me that this woman had the perception that her church didn't care about what she did in her work life. She assumed that what she does outside the church doesn't count. I'm pretty sure that if we went to her congregation (or any of ours, for that matter) and asked leaders or members if this woman's work is important, we would get resounding affirmation. But if we asked what her congregation (or ours) had done to affirm or support her day-to-day ministry, we would probably

---

1. DuBois, "Walgreens," 17–20. This story, along with much of the first half of this chapter, was first published in the Alban Institute's magazine.

get puzzled looks. Why do we let such wonderful ministry slip through our fingers, unnoticed and unsupported?

This chapter tells the story of conversations that I first had with pastors, which were followed by visits with members in a variety of congregations. We will first consider what pastors say about ministry in daily life and why it doesn't often appear on their or their congregations' radars. The pastors are insightful and helpful, and they open the door to the realities we face. But, as we will find, theirs is only one side of the story. The perceptions of the members are startlingly different from those of the pastors. In the end, though, we will find that both viewpoints share a pronounced degree of vagueness and lack of certainty about the ministry to which all of God's people are called in their baptism.

LISTENING TO THE PASTORS

The seeds for this book were planted several years ago when I started a project designed to answer one question: *How might we describe, empower, and support pastors who see their calling in terms of equipping members for ministry in their everyday lives?* The project began when a nearby pastor asked me to put together a book study on what it means to be an equipping pastor. She had in mind the passage from Ephesians 4:11–12, "The gifts he gave were that some would be apostles, some prophets, some evangelists, some pastors and teachers, to equip the saints for the work of ministry, for building up the body of Christ." The request was simple and exciting.

A few months later, after reading the first batch of books that came to my attention, I had discovered plenty of books aimed at helping people find their calling in life, I found other books that talked about how pastors should and could train the laity for leadership *in the church*, but I found no books designed to help pastors focus their ministry on equipping people for their callings *in the world*. Now I was even more intrigued, and somewhat puzzled.

This apparent dead end led to what was called the Equipping Pastors project. I wanted to know: What does it mean to be an equipping pastor? How is that different from what most pastors are trained to be and do? What are the implications of this for program, staff, structure, and day-to-day operation of a congregation? How does one shift from being a caretaker or program pastor to being an equipping pastor?

With these questions identified, I sent out a letter to about 140 pastors in the judicatory I am a part of, telling them about this discovery. I invited them to a one-time, ninety-minute conversation to discuss the above questions. I hoped six to twelve pastors would accept my invitation. I was astonished when fifty-eight pastors turned out for the first round of conversations. Over the following year I scheduled additional conversations, eventually including well over one hundred pastors from six denominations.

What I learned from these pastors is summarized below. (The full report and a study guide are available on www.TheScattering.org.) I cannot provide uniform results (there were none), or the opinion of a majority. Nor can I provide percentages of pastors who fall into any given category since these were small group conversations that, while they were structured the same, were not all the same. I can describe discoveries and observations in broad strokes, and I use actual comments from participants to illuminate the findings. The anonymity of respondents has been intentionally maintained.

INTENSELY INTERESTED YET UNSURE WHAT TO DO

One of the most obvious findings that came out of these conversations is that pastors are intensely interested in being equipping pastors; the large number of pastors who participated is evidence of that. To have nearly half of the pastors in our judicatory express an interest in this topic was simply stunning. When asked why they had responded to the invitation to participate, I heard comments such as the following: "I have a passion for this topic." "It's a key area of congregational health." "There is a crying need to work on this."

At the same time there was a palpable sense—and many admitted it—that pastors are unsure what it means to be an equipping pastor, or to take steps to become one. They told me, "Equipping people for ministry *is* our job, but we don't get much help with how to do it." "We've been trained how to do ministry in and for the church, but we've not gone beyond that." And perhaps most piercing was the comment, "I've been a paid Christian for so long that I no longer remember what it is like to be a Christian in the world."

It is encouraging that so many pastors are interested in this topic. It is also encouraging that pastors are willing to admit their sense of inadequacy and even failure. Confessing that the power of the priesthood of all believers has not been fully unleashed is the first step toward bringing about change.

AWARENESS OF SYSTEMIC BLOCKS

The second significant finding from the conversations is that pastors are acutely aware of systems, structures, and cultural understandings that keep us from becoming as good at the scattering as we are at the gathering. The pastors talked about these blocks in detail and with considerable emotion; these were, after all, the things that keep them from doing what they feel called to do.

It takes ordination to be a minister

The stumbling block that was often mentioned first is the common (mis)understanding that pastors "do ministry" and congregational members partake of it. Common statements include: "The people want me to do everything." "Ministry is the pastor's job at my church." Or, "People come to church to consume a product, be it music, preaching, or community." While some rebelled against this misunderstanding (in the words of one, "I can tell you what ministry is not: 'I'm in charge of everything.' That's not ministry!"), pastors admitted buying into this systemic expectation to justify their existence, to keep people happy, and to assure the continual flow of paychecks. Comments included, "Pastors succumb to congregational expectations to 'do ministry.' Congregations hire pastors to do ministry and the people follow. People might manage big companies, but when they come to the church they look to the pastor for direction in everything." One pastor who was called to a specialized ministry in a congregation said, "I arrived and the people working in that area were relieved, thinking, 'Now we don't have to do anything.' Now I'm watching people leave, claiming that their reason for dissatisfaction is that I'm not doing my job." Author Sue Mallory put it this way: "Pastors end up taking on all kind of roles and tasks, even if they're ill equipped to perform them, simply because they accept the understanding that 'it's what they pay me for!' "[2] The authors of *The Equipping Pastor* describe the dampening effect of the commodification of ministry: "The hire-and-fire mentality of the North American society has

2. Mallory, *Equipping Church*, 40–41.

reduced the pastor's ministry to a buy-and-sell commodity. A pastor with a vision to equip all the members for ministry . . . is apt to run into the mentality, 'We hired *you* to do the ministry.' "[3]

Unfortunately, the understanding that pastor = minister and minister = pastor is embedded deep in our DNA. When someone discerns a call to ordination, we talk about her or him "going into the ministry." When there is a crisis situation, we want "the minister" to be present, and we overlook family members and friends who also provide valid ministry to the one in crisis. On a conference call between leaders of several of our seminaries, the person leading the meeting—a seminary professor—opened with prayer, asking God's blessing on our meeting, on the seminaries we represent, and on the students, who (speaking to God) "will be your ministers in the world."

Institutional survival trumps all

A second systemic block mentioned by pastors is that ministry is largely seen as something that happens within the gathered church because of intense pressure to keep the institution alive. In an age of declining institutions across society, the pressure is enormous to keep the congregation healthy or even to bring it back to what it used to be. Pastors said things like, "The structure (that is, the institution) keeps us from enacting the vision and hopes that called us to pursue ordination in the first place." Or, "Pastors want to equip people for ministry in daily life, but the people want us to be chaplains." In short, keeping the doors open becomes our primary focus because of pressure to maintain the institution. Focusing on our life as the scattered church doesn't stand a chance of getting a hearing because it has no measurable payback for the institution.

In a casual conversation after the first eleven gatherings, one pastor who was unable to attend expressed a desire to have been part of the gatherings because of the perceived difficulty of identifying and training congregational leaders. When reminded that the focus of the conversations was about equipping members for ministry in the world, this pastor replied, "But I need leaders in the congregation too!"

Don't get me wrong—congregations need qualified and equipped leaders. As gathered church, we need Sunday school teachers, worship leaders, grounds crews, small group leaders, and a host of other volunteers.

---

3. Stevens and Collins, *Equipping Pastor*, 2. Emphasis in original.

It is important to stoke the fires of the organization. But in the vast majority of congregations, these needs become the end itself instead of the means. In the words of Davida Foy Crabtree,

> *Form does not follow function. The church exists for mission, for the sake of the world. Yet it is organized to build itself up as an institution. It draws people to itself, but fails to send them back out. It blesses the work its members do within the institution, but pays no attention to the work they do "outside" the church.*[4]

What counts in our institution-centric way of thinking is what our members do *in*, *for*, and *through* the gathered church—and if we're forward thinking, how we can attract more people to join us. We value Sunday school teachers, board members, Bible study participants, choir members, and food pantry workers—we call them active members. These are the people and activities that we can count. And count them we do because those numbers tell us whether we're successful, if we're growing, and how effective our leaders are.

The split between Sunday and Monday

The third major systemic block that pastors described is the lack of connection between what people do at church and what they do in the world, or in popular usage, the split between Sunday and Monday. Bill Diehl's books in the eighties and nineties (e.g., *Thank God It's Monday*) and others like them have drilled into our consciousness the gap between what happens on Sunday and what we do during the rest of the week. We talk about the gap easily and frequently. It seems that there is a steady stream of reports that repeat what the World Council of Churches declared in 1948: "[M]illions of people think of the Church as floating above the modern world and entirely out of touch with it."[5] In more contemporary terms we are told that people are leaving the church or not even giving the church a chance because "what happens there has no connection to my life."

It was easy for the pastors in these early conversations to elaborate on the split between Sunday and Monday. "Our people struggle with faith in society. But we all know that we're not supposed to talk about sex, politics, or money!" "People want both a 'spiritual world' and a 'real world.' In my

---

4. Crabtree, *Empowering Church*, xii. Emphasis in original.

5. *Evanston Speaks*, 104.

congregation, when we first began to deal with this, there was resistance to admitting this was true. I felt I was going to be run out of town for raising the question."

Chris Scharen puts it this way:

> Religion is at best one piece of a busy life, perhaps impacting one's "soul" or "heart" as a means to help cope with the hectic pace of the rest of life, where other values rule. . . . In such a vision of modern life, love of neighbor may rule the soul, but love of a bargain rules in shopping, love of taste and beauty rules in the arts, and so on. In giving our allegiance to these various sphere-centered values, we in a sense make them gods . . . [M]ost churches and pastoral leaders have accepted the demotion to one sphere of life — that of things "spiritual."[6]

Other systemic blocks

In addition to the three major categories reported above, pastors also reported other factors that hinder their ability to balance the gathered and scattered expressions of the church. While these were not mentioned frequently, they are worth including here.

The busyness of pastors and members leads to a sense of paralysis. "Length of commitment is a problem for busy people." "Most people think that they only need to come to worship at my church. They'll volunteer for worship tasks, but little outside of that." Since the Equipping Pastors conversations, I've noticed how persistent the theme of busyness is, and I've heard several people lament how it's destroying the church. I often hear pastors say, "I can't ask my members to do anything more. They're already so busy; the church just can't burden them further."

In addition to busyness, some pastors talked about a growing awareness of the difference in expectations between older generations and younger generations. "Boomers called me to be the 'program' pastor, but younger people don't want programs, so I feel crappy. We are experiencing the breakdown between the Boomer church (that expects programs) and the next generation." Another said, "My frustration with ministry in daily life is that I have to talk to people in the 'church culture' (who pay the bills) and people who inhabit the 'tech society' (who see community in Facebook) at the same time, and that is hard."

---

6. Scharen, *Way of Life*, 15, 24.

And finally, one comment summarized what often happens in the face of such systemic blocks: "Pastors retreat to their comfort zones, and ministry in daily life is not one of them."

CONFUSION ABOUT THE NATURE OF MINISTRY

The third significant finding from the conversations with pastors is that there is considerable confusion about what it means to be a scattered church. In most cases, our conversations about ministry in daily life were restricted by confusion about what *ministry* is. This confusion was expressed in terms of both internal and external understandings of ministry.

Internal confusion

In addition to the finding above ("It takes ordination to be a minister") that ministry is often restricted to what pastors do, the pastors also reported that when members are encouraged to find their ministry, at best it is limited to what they can or should do in and through the gathered church. Pastors pointed out that inventories used to recruit members for ministry are often restricted to how they can serve within the gathered church and to some degree how they can serve the world through their congregation's outreach ministry.

Pastors also named the reality that ministry is often confused with what it takes to maintain a congregation. Speaking from the context of a congregation that was struggling to survive, one pastor defined ministry as "the need to survive as an institution." One pastor said, "I think institutionally we focus on keeping the machine alive." In another instance, a pastor said, "We get caught up in needing to keep people in worship, or attracting more people to worship, in order to keep the building in shape and the bills paid." A few pastors, sometimes pointedly, had a hard time grasping that ministry could or should be an external activity.

External confusion

Even when we shift our attention to the scattered church, our understanding of ministry is less than it could be. Pastors reported hearing their members speak about ministry in daily life only as a matter of being nice or moral, as being faithful to friends or coworkers, not engaging in gossip, or speaking of having gone to worship or on a mission trip. One pastor offered, "When I ask people about how their faith is active in their daily life, I get back stories of working in volunteer positions."

One pastor described a prior call that included the task of equipping members for ministry. The work was focused, not just on filling the congregation's volunteer slots, but on making a concerted effort to "tap their gifts in the world," which, in this case, meant filling slots for volunteer organizations in the community. That is commendable, and certainly reaches further than many congregations. But when I asked this pastor how the congregation helps accountants understand their ministry, the first response was "that wasn't always their ministry giftedness." The second response was, "we didn't address how to live faith in daily life."

Clearly, everything the pastors reported is part of what it means to live out our baptismal calling, but somehow it doesn't quite add up to the vision that the woman at Walgreens lives out.

LOSING TOUCH WITH THE WORLD

The opening biblical exploration/devotion time for these conversations centered on Ephesians 4:11–13. That passage begins, "The gifts he gave were that some would be apostles, some prophets, some evangelists, some pastors and teachers, to equip the saints for the work of ministry, for building up the body of Christ." The intent was to focus on the work of "equipping the saints for the work of ministry," but one cannot do that without also considering the next phrase, "for building up the body of Christ."

The conversations, at least in part, revealed that our diminished understanding of the scattered church may be rooted in the fact that pastors spend the majority of their time in the church, working to build up the Body of Christ (as they should), but in so doing they lose touch with life in the world.

Perhaps a personal confession will help: Soon after beginning work as the director of the Center for Renewal at Grand View University, I began introducing myself as a "recovering parish pastor." It was meant to be a humorous introduction, but as time passed I realized that I was indeed recovering from my addiction to parish ministry. In short, I came to realize that my life had been wholly consumed by the work to which I had been called. I ate, drank, and breathed the church. Please hear this: I'm not saying that the work I did, or that pastors do, is unimportant. It is vitally important. What I'm saying is that I lost my perspective; things got out of balance, and I became disconnected from life in—I'm sorry, I don't know another way to put this—I became disconnected from life in the real world.

This all came into sharp focus during the first year at the Center for Renewal. For twenty-five years I had been frustrated and dumbfounded (and when I'm really honest, angry) with parishioners who didn't attend Holy Week services. During that first Holy Week outside of the parish, my wife and I attended Maundy Thursday services, as was our custom. But at 7:00 pm on Good Friday I found myself standing in the kitchen of our home. The memory is so vivid, the shock was so great, that I could show you the exact spot where I was standing when this happened. "Oh my gosh!" I exclaimed to my wife, "We forgot about Good Friday services!" My next—and immediate—thought was revelation: *So this is how it happens? People have a life that doesn't center around the church.*

In the process of focusing on the gathered church, pastors often forget that those who have not been set aside for our particular task spend their lives as the scattered church. Pastors, perhaps rightly, focus on the ministry that happens in and through the church. In the process, though, we forget that ministry also happens in the farm field, where food is grown so that people might be fed. Ministry happens in classrooms, where children and adults receive education necessary for their welfare and for the sake of the world. Ministry happens when parents change a diaper, clothe, feed, shelter, and raise their children. Ministry happens when adult children care for aging parents. Ministry happens in civic roles (e.g., police, military, legal, or political) when evil is resisted and justice, equality, and fairness are promoted. Ministry happens in the workplace where products are produced, where countless decisions are made, where people and all creation are protected and served.

To that end, the church exists as God's people, gathered to be forgiven and fed, prepared, empowered, and then scattered in service to the world.

IT'S FUNNY HOW THINGS WORK OUT

After the initial round of eleven conversations, I wrote an interim report and then held two lunches to report back to the pastors what I had heard from them. Overwhelmingly they told me that I had heard them correctly, and they expressed appreciation for being heard. They said it was also helpful to hear that others felt and experienced many of the same things they had. The funny thing I want to point out is that at the second lunch one pastor urged me to stop calling this the Equipping Pastors project. He noted that doing so only puts the focus back on the pastor, which is antithetical to its purpose. I took that comment to heart and started calling it the Equipping Congregations project.

Then a second funny thing happened: another pastor raised the possibility of involving lay people in this conversation. This pastor asked, "What would lay people say an equipping pastor is?"

Okay, so these two points are not comically funny. But they are interesting twists that set us up well for the next stage of this journey. After working with pastors for a year and a half, it was time to engage the people in the pews in conversation. I was confident I had a handle on things because the pastors had described in great detail what was going on in their congregations. I trusted that information because pastors are the experts on congregational life, and they couldn't be wrong, could they?

TESTING THE RESULTS—AND BEING BLOWN AWAY

I set up a series of forums in congregations to hear what the people had to say. How did they perceive ministry? Were the pastors right in believing that their people would resist their efforts to broaden their congregations to include the ministry they do in their daily lives? I began each forum by asking participants to say what comes to mind when they hear these words or phrases:

Ministry

Ministry of the laity

Ministry of all the baptized

The priesthood of all believers

Minister

Vocation

Ministry in daily life

I planned to record their responses on a white board or flip chart. When we finished this word association exercise, I intended to identify patterns and themes that would reveal the (mis)understandings of ministry the pastors had reported that their members have. I was confident that their answers would show that members restrict *ministry* to what pastors do, or at best to what members can or should do in and through the gathered church. Then to drive my point home I intended to ask three questions to unveil their limited understanding:

What does this reveal about our assumptions about ministry?

Who does ministry?

Where does ministry take place?

While the questions don't sound terribly pointed, in my plan they were not only pointed, they had a serrated edge. Based on the frustration I had heard from the pastors, I wanted to convict the people of their misunderstanding at best and their failure at worst. Having proved myself to be an amazing and convincing sleuth, the rest of the forum would go on to consider better approaches.

When the first forum started I whipped out my list and the dry erase markers and dove in. By the time the word association exercise was over, though, my plan was shot full of holes. My notes from the first forum read, "The participants were not nearly as 'pastors do ministry' or 'ministry is something that happens in the church' as I expected. In fact, they had a good handle on ministry." But, I told myself, this congregation was an exception to the rule. It's large and bustling; I was sure I would find what I was looking for in the other congregations.

I couldn't have been more mistaken. Every congregation I visited—large or small, urban, suburban or rural, thriving or declining—followed the pattern of the first congregation. In the opening word association exercise at each forum, the people expressed an understanding that they are God's people in the world, loving and serving others. I never got to use my pointed questions—even once.

It did happen, though it was rare, that someone referred to ministry as "what the pastor does." In one church, "Ministry of the laity" was defined as "supporting the pastor." In two forums, the first response to "Minister" was "Pastor." Overwhelmingly, though, forum participants defined ministry as "spreading the Word of God," "service," "giving," or "helping others." At one congregation, one participant identified the pattern at the end of the word association exercise this way: "There are lots of ways to serve God. This is about who you are in relationship to the world; how you fit into the world. It's about your mission. It's a matter of being a reflection of Christ's light."

Even though the word association exercise never gave me the "Ah ha! See how you miss the point?" moment that I anticipated, I continued with the lesson plan. After reviewing their responses (and skipping over my pointed questions), I had them read 1 Peter 4:2–3, 8–11, about "maintaining constant love for one another, being hospitable to one another, serving one another with whatever gift each of you has received, as one who is speaking the very words of God." I intended to ask, "If ministry is a matter of what pastors do or what happens in the church, what does First Peter have to say about ministry and where it takes place?" In every forum I wound up having to shorten the question to "What does First Peter have to say about ministry and where it takes place?" I heard answers like, "There is no separation between one's life and ministry." "It takes place everywhere." "Ministry happens in daily life." "Do what God is calling you to do." "Ministry happens from the time you get up in the morning to when you go to bed."

Interestingly, a participant in one forum said, "We can reach people that the clergy cannot. Laity together have wider reach." In another forum the response was, "Some people see ministry as a matter of 'What we do when we have time to do something for someone.' But ministry is more a matter of what we don't plan. It comes upon us. It's a reflection of who we are. Think of all the things you do as a parent. It's an attitude of living a life of service to and for others."

Later in the forum I had the participants read Ephesians 4:4–7, 11–13 with its well-known phrase, "equip the saints for the work of ministry." I asked what they noticed about the passage, what was a new insight, or what spoke to them. The participants responded with statements like "We all have gifts and talents and responsibilities to go out and share." I pressed on with my torpedoed plan, asking whether this passage is directed at an internal church activity or to an external activity. "Both" was the most common answer.

In the next part of the forum I offered a brief introduction to the findings from the pastors. At one site, someone interrupted my presentation to tell me they disagreed with the pastors. Others in the group nodded in agreement. They told me that pastors *are* equippers, they just don't know that they are. "They shouldn't need evidence. Being an equipping pastor can be compared to parenting, that is, equipping children for life. How many parents know they're doing things right? How many know what they are doing? We may not see evidence for a long time."

It was during the presentation of the findings from the pastors, though, that some windows for conversation opened. One person responded to the report by admitting, "We leave church on Sunday and leave faith behind. We go back into the world and operate by a different set of rules." Another participant said, "I need to feel empowered for ministry, but I don't feel empowered by my congregation."

At the end of the forums I asked, "How might your pastor's job description change if we took this charge to equip people for ministry in their daily lives seriously?" I also asked, "How might your congregation change if pastors did what they feel called to do?" Responses included: "Equipping should be foremost in the job description." "We need to flip expectations upside down regarding who does what. The people do the ministry, and the pastor supports what they do."

In summary: the lay people I encountered[7] said pretty much the exact opposite of what the pastors said. To my surprise, they reported a clear awareness that they are doing ministry in their everyday lives, and they want to be equipped and empowered for that ministry, but many feel they are not getting that. I finished those forums wondering, How could pastors and their people be reading each other so differently?

A LESS THAN CLEAR UNDERSTANDING OF MINISTRY

Having reported the surprising findings from the forums, it's now necessary to offer something of a contradiction. Even though the members I talked to see ministry as being broader than what pastors describe, there was still a pervasive sense of vagueness about what ministry in the world looks like. Even though they said that ministry happens "from the time you get up in the morning to when you go to bed," a lingering sense of uncertainty hung over the conversations. As surprised as I was by the reports that people

---

7. In all, I talked to nearly 300 lay people in the forums that I conducted. It should be noted that I may have been "preaching to the choir." The members I talked to were those who are willing to attend adult forums, which in most congregations is a small percentage of people, and people who are probably more attuned to the life of the congregation. If I could have found a way to talk with people who only attend worship (or even those who infrequently attend worship) I may have heard responses more in line with what I was expecting. But hearing from "the choir" is still encouraging; it tells us that there are people in our congregations who "get it" and who are desirous of being more intentional about equipping them for the work of ministry.

know that they are called to ministry in daily life, I left with the distinct impression that they have a hard time describing it.

This finding was clarified for me when I had the opportunity to preach on Mark 6. In this part of Mark's gospel, the disciples had just returned from what we would call a mission trip. At the beginning of the chapter they had been sent out two by two, with authority over the unclean spirits. Mark reports that when they returned they excitedly reported the stunning success of their first attempts at ministering in Jesus' name. I wonder what the first century equivalent of high-fives or fist bumps was, because they were most certainly doing that.

A few verses later, with the crowds in hot pursuit, Mark reports that the disciples started whining. "It's getting late," they tell Jesus. "Can't we just send them away? We need some rest." But Jesus tells them to give the crowds something to eat. He seems to imply, "You just worked miracles; do it again." But the disciples fail to understand and ask, "Are we going to spend 200 days' wages to buy food for them?"

What happened to the disciples? Just a few verses earlier they had been successful colleagues in Jesus' work. They had changed from being followers to participants, from disciples to apostles (that is, from students to "sent ones"), from watchers to doers. Before the story is over, the disciples are back to being groupies, hangers-on—mere busboys picking up the dirty dishes after everyone had eaten.

After retelling this story, I asked the people, "What is it that keeps you from living and serving as God's people in the world?" I had them break into pairs or trios to talk, asking them to boil down their response to a single word or phrase, write it on a sticky note, and then walk to the front and stick their response to the cross.

What happened next surprised me greatly. As I helped people place their stickies on the cross I started to see patterns. Even though I had no plans to do anything with these sticky note confessions, I quickly saw that I needed to collect their responses and study them. The word cloud on page 36 emerged:

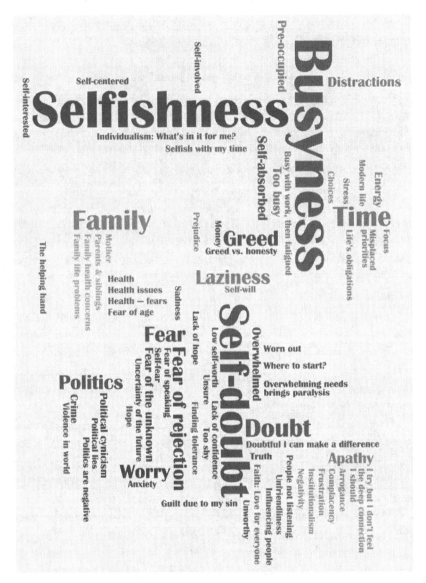

Word cloud summarizing reasons why people feel unable to be God's people at work in the world.

In a word cloud, the larger the word is, the more frequently it was mentioned. In this image, only one person wrote the smallest words; about thirty people mentioned the largest words. In normal word clouds the words are arranged randomly; in this case I created clusters to show relationships between the words and phrases.[8]

The one response that surprised me the most is in the Family cluster and it reads, simply, "Mother." There are many ways that that one word could be explained, but my assumption is that this is from an adult who cares for an elderly mother. The other individual responses in this cluster are similar: parents and siblings, family health concerns, family life problems, or (as several indicated) simply "family." What I started to see as people stuck their responses to the cross was confirmed by the word cloud: *In many cases people feel that the very people and tasks to which God calls them as care-givers, servants, or ministers are keeping them from being God's people at work in the world.* That is an interesting and a puzzling disconnect, isn't it?

It wouldn't be much of a leap to see this same disconnect in the largest cluster in the word cloud: busyness. When asked, most of us will say that we don't waste our time—at least not much of it. Sure, we'll sit to watch television, catch up on Facebook, or read a book, but most of our busyness involves tasks that are important either to our own health and well-being, the welfare of our families and communities, or the success of our workplace. Even so-called "wasteful" leisure activities, such as those identified in the previous sentence, can be helpful to our health and well-being, to the health and well-being of our relationships with others, or both. By and large, even in our busyness we are tending to the various callings—be they personal, family, work, or community—to which God calls us. To quote Luther, "There is no work better than another to please God; to pour water, to wash dishes, to be a shoemaker, or an apostle, all are one, as touching the deed, to please God."[9] The same argument could potentially be made for the other large cluster, selfishness, but admittedly that connection might be a little more tenuous. While self-absorption can be the very definition of sin, quite often in our preoccupation with all of our tasks and responsibilities we are still tending to the callings given to us by God.

Matthew 25 tells the familiar story of the judgment of the sheep and the goats. Have you ever considered the reaction of the sheep, the righteous

---

8. In the interest of transparency, I may have unintentionally tainted my sample: In giving instructions for this exercise I offered an example: "For instance, if I was going to write down one thing right now that blocks me from being involved in the world, I would say 'political cynicism.'" The "politics" group in the lower left corner may have been different or even absent if I had not given my example.

9. Luther, "Treatise on Good Works, 1520," *LW* 44, 26–27

ones? "Lord, when was it that we saw you hungry or thirsty or as a stranger or naked or sick or in prison?" The sheep were doing ministry; *they just didn't realize it.*

We are a lot like the sheep: we miss the fact that our families, work, busyness, and maybe even our selfishness are avenues for God-given ministry. Even worse, we see these things as keeping us from being God's people at work in the world.

THE SOURCE OF OUR MISUNDERSTANDING OF CALL

Having identified the vagueness that undermines our understanding of ministry as the scattered church, I set out to discover its source. In particular I wondered, "How did the people get the relatively clear understanding that they are, indeed, called to ministry in the world?" and "Why is that understanding vague and uncertain?"

Over the months that followed the adult forums, I found myself observing all that we do in our congregations with a new set of lenses. I was watching and listening for references to ministry as the scattered church. At first I wondered whether the (mis)understandings of ministry reported earlier could be attributed to the fact that there just aren't enough references to it in our congregations. Once again, what I found went totally against what I expected. Wearing my new scattered church glasses, I was amazed by how often there are references to it in our worship services. It cropped up in prayers, in liturgical responses, in hymns, in Scripture, and sermons.

For example, in preparation for a small group that I was going to lead on a Monday, I went through the worship order from the day before and found the following items:

- In one of our hymns we sang, "You touch us through physicians' skills, through nurses' gifts of care, and through the love of faithful friends who lift our lives in prayer."[10]

- The following phrases were used in the prayers:

  - Free us to boldly proclaim the gospel.

  - Uphold the oppressed, liberate those in bondage . . . free us to work for justice and peace.

  - Sustain the poor and hungry, heal those who are ill or afflicted.

10. "We Come to You for Healing, Lord," by Herman G. Stuempfle Jr. © 2002 GIA Publications, Inc. All rights reserved.

- Free us to be your hands of love and compassion.
- Save us from lives and schedules filled with too much activity.

- In part, the prayer following communion asked, "Send us now as your disciples, announcing peace and proclaiming that the reign of God has come near."

- At the end of the service the pastor said, "Go in peace. Proclaim the good news."[11]

When I developed this particular list I was disappointed because it was shorter than what I considered normal, based on recent observations. But even as short as this list is, it illustrates that the references to scattered ministries are to be found in our congregational life, frequently and consistently.

In fact, such references are everywhere. For instance, there is a list of expectations for the life and involvement of what is called a "faithful member" in the Presbyterian *Book of Order*. After listing six items that talk mostly about life within a congregation (e.g., worship, study of Scripture, giving money and time), the last three items talk about life and ministry in the world. Such involvement includes:

- responding to God's activity in the world through service to others;

- living responsibly in the personal, family, vocational, political, cultural, and social relationships of life; and,

- working in the world for peace, justice, freedom, and human fulfillment.[12]

These expectations are remarkably similar to the commitment asked of confirmands and new members in the Lutheran liturgy. In part, the Affirmation of Baptism liturgy asks, "Do you intend to continue in the covenant God made with you in holy baptism . . . to proclaim the good news of God in Christ through word and deed, to serve all people, following the example of Jesus, and to strive for justice and peace in all the earth?"[13]

---

11. All of these phrases came from http://members.sundaysandseasons.com, in the "Day Texts" section.

12. *Book of Order*, G-1.0304, 21.

13. *ELW*, 237. There is a similar list of expectations in question and answer form in the 1977 Episcopalian *Book of Common Prayer*, p. 417. See also Prentiss and Lowe, *Radical Sending*, 22–28, for a thorough examination of the components of the *Book of Common Prayer* that speak to scattering of the church.

Looking in the United Methodist hymnal, one of the liturgies for Word and Table offers this prayer following communion: "Eternal God, we give you thanks for this holy mystery in which you have given yourself to us. Grant that we may go into the world in the strength of your Spirit, to give ourselves for others."[14] Likewise, the confession from the Service of Word and Table, Rite II, says, "[W]e have not loved our neighbors, and we have not heard the cry of the needy. . . . Free us for joyful obedience."[15] The baptismal liturgy asks, "According to the grace given to you, will you . . . serve as Christ's representatives in the world?"[16]

This brief review of examples does not include the large number of hymns that affirm the variety of ways that "We all are called for service, to witness in God's name. Our ministries are different; our purpose is the same: to touch the lives of others with God's surprising grace, so ev'ry folk and nation may feel God's warm embrace."[17] We share many of these hymns across denominational lines and to do a review of them would take up more space than is necessary. All you need to do is put on scattered church glasses for the next few weeks and see how many times hymns call God's people to ministry in the world. The references are plentiful if only we have eyes to see and ears to hear.

Which is exactly what the case seems to be: Our people do have the eyes to see and the ears to hear. They have heard the prayers, the liturgical commitments, the hymns, and the scriptural imperatives to love and serve our neighbor. This could very well explain how the people in the forums were able to torpedo my best-laid plans. But what explains the vagueness, the lingering sense of uncertainty that came out of the forums, and the confused responses that are shown in the word cloud? How could it be that people can report that caring for family members keeps them from being God's people at work in the world?

A CLOSER LOOK AT OUR PRACTICE

As many times as I have proved my assumptions to be wrong, I stand open to the possibility that what I am about to say is wrong as well, but I don't

14. *UMH*, 11.

15. Ibid., 12.

16. Ibid., 34.

17. "We All Are One in Mission," by Rusty Edwards. © 1986 Hope Publishing Company, Carol Stream, IL 60188. All rights reserved.

think it is. Another observation that came from looking at our communal life with scattered church glasses is that many of the references listed above are made in general terms. We consistently talk about feeding the hungry, serving the poor, speaking for justice and the like, but *rarely do we ground those phrases in concrete terms*. As we leave, many liturgies send worshipers into the world with words like, "Go in peace, serve the Lord," or "The worship is ended; the service begins," but we rarely connect such phrases with concrete examples. We preach about the Good Samaritan and urge people to be selfless and loving, but we don't often illustrate that love with stories from real people and actual places where such selfless love has been shown. We pray that the hungry may be fed, but too often we unwittingly leave that task in God's hands, as if God is going to once again rain down manna so that all people may eat.

Earlier I referred to preparing to lead a small group discussion on ministry in daily life. It was at that gathering that one of the participants reflected on his work in a way that apparently he had never done before. Thinking out loud he said, "I should link my work of financing farm equipment to the call to feed the hungry. Do I make that connection? Not as much as I should." The larger question is whether, prior to our gathering, he should have been expected to make that connection on his own. It wasn't until our small group conversation challenged him to consider the connection between faith and his work that he saw his work as a concrete expression of the biblical command to feed the hungry. Over the course of all the years that this man had been in church, it appears that nobody had helped him make the connection between our categorical imperatives to feed the hungry and the concrete reality that in his professional life he is doing just that.

SO WHAT DO WE TALK ABOUT?

Earlier we looked at the parable of the sheep and goats in Matthew 25. Why didn't the sheep see that they had been ministering in Christ's name? Why do we look at the roles, relationships, and responsibilities of our everyday lives as being in competition with our call to be God's people at work in the world? Maybe that is because we value above all else what our members do in and for the gathered church. It's as if Matthew 25 says: "Then the king will say to those at his right hand, 'Come, you that are blessed by my Father, inherit the kingdom prepared for you from the foundation of the world;

for I offered a worship service and you attended, I asked you to serve on a committee and you said yes, I needed a Sunday school teacher and you volunteered.' "

Being accustomed to using gathered church glasses, we are very adept at giving concrete examples of living out our faith as something that happens in or through the congregation's ministry. We are intentional about helping both current and new members find their place in the ministries of the congregation. We are not as well acquainted with viewing our work through scattered church glasses, and often fail to help them identify their ministry at home or at work.

It would be nice to be able to place blame for our persistent focus on gathered church ministries in someone's lap. But all the evidence points to the fact that this is a mutually reinforced expectation. It is as if pastors have blinders on that keep their focus squarely on the survival or the vitality of the congregation. Speaking for myself here, as I admitted earlier, when I was in the parish I ate, drank, and breathed the church. When I talked with members, we usually wound up talking about the church.

On the other hand, it is apparent that members also expect to focus on the church. They expect pastors to focus on the church because that is what they are paid to do. Members instinctively know that when we're at church we do churchy things. We know that when we leave the church, our focus will return to our family, work, leisure, and community involvements.

> With most of their activities away from the church building, lay members see the congregation as a belonging group with whom they gather occasionally for support, spiritual nourishment and doing good works. They want their congregations to continue to be stable, comfortable places. They have some sense of responsibility for their church, but recognize it as one of many demands on their time, money and talents. Their lives are focused on doing their daily work well. Scattered in the world, members try to carry out Christian ideals in their personal lives, but see little connection between their church membership and their daily tasks.[18]

As it turns out, our pervasive gathered church orientation does not come from one side or the other. In this case, neither the chicken nor the egg came first. It's just the way things are. Holding nothing back, Judith McWilliams Dickhart summarizes our situation on page 1 of her book:

---

18. McWilliams Dickhart, *Church-going Insider*, 15. Emphasis in original.

[Congregations put almost all their attention on] developing active, involved church-goers. Leaders may hope that what happens inside a church will rub off on members, but they do not use the time inside to prepare members to carry the Gospel into the world.

In fact, members have come to expect *the church* to be the locus for mission, not *the world*. Many leave worship believing they have fulfilled the church's expectations of them. They are pretty much on their own to figure out how to lead a Christian life the rest of the week.[19]

ONE MORE REASON FOR THE DISCONNECT

There is yet one more reason for our inability to describe our scattered ministries in concrete terms: *we look at ministry as a matter of doing something extra*. In fact, this may be the most significant reason we have found so far.

Over the course of this journey it has become apparent that most of us—pastors and members alike—assume that ministry is a matter of doing something in addition to everything else we're already doing. Why else would we list *family* as something that keeps us from being God's people at work in the world? We see our obligations and our day-to-day responsibilities as competition for the ministry opportunities that we promote at church because ministry is something extra that we do—if we have the interest and the time. This is precisely why "busyness" shows up as an obstacle to ministry.

What if we stopped looking at ministry as a program that can only thrive if we ask people to do something more? I'm speaking primarily to pastors here, but other congregational leaders and members can join in with this exercise. What might happen if, instead of seeing our jobs principally as a matter of lining up volunteers for the congregation's classes, committees, or projects, we started looking at leadership in terms of supporting, equipping, encouraging, and sending people for the many ministries that they are already involved in when we are scattered?

Consider these two contrasting stories:

On Sunday morning in late August the pastor opens worship with announcements.[20] And, of course, being late August there is a pitch for filling

---

19. Ibid., 1. Emphasis in original.

20. I'm not making this story up. This actually occurred in a church that I visited. The second story was told to me in the first person during my first round of Equipping

the last two slots for Sunday school teachers. In order to add urgency to the request, the pastor says, "I hope you'll consider teaching one of these classes; it's one of the most important ministries you'll ever perform in your life." While it is true that Sunday school teachers are important, while they play a vital role in our congregations, and while it is certainly true that we need people to teach, is it really one of the most important ministries that we can undertake? Is it more important than raising a child, or planting and harvesting a crop so that the hungry can be fed? Is it more important than simply being present for a friend who is suffering emotionally?

Now put yourself in this pastor's shoes: It's late August when a pastor approaches a member who has been identified as a potential teacher for one of those open slots. The member listens to the request and regretfully replies, "I'd love to do that, Pastor, but I just can't take on anything more right now. I have kids at home who demand a lot of my time, and I am caring for my mother, who is suffering from dementia. I hate to tell you this, but I can't do it." The pastor replies, "That's your ministry right now. Take care of your children and your mom, and let us know if we can do anything to support you in those roles. I'll find somebody else to teach this class."

Which pastor (or congregational leader) are you? Which would you rather be? Which approach would be more fulfilling?

No doubt, some of you are thinking, "I want to be a leader who has a full roster of Sunday school teachers *and* a passion to support members for their ministry in daily life." So would I. But what has happened is that, because of the pervasive sense that institutional needs and vitality trumps all, many of us live the first pastor's story and forget the second. Moving toward becoming an equipping congregation—and I'm getting ahead of myself a little here but I'll finish the thought—means putting ministry *in the world* at the center of our self-understanding (both personally and corporately) and seeing ministry *in the church* as vital and necessary, not simply as an end in and of itself, but for the encouragement, equipping, and empowering of all God's people.

Pastors conversations.

PUTTING ALL THIS TOGETHER

Over the past few years, as I watched, read, listened, and observed, I gathered more and more information. As a result, I found it increasingly difficult to explain to people what I discovered in the confines of a brief conversation. After I finished the conversations with both pastors and members, I developed the following chart in an attempt to boil down what I found to a concise description.

On the one hand . . .	On the other hand . . .
We promote ministry in daily life a lot—in liturgy, hymns, prayers, and sermons.	We use general, categorical terms (feed the poor, work for peace) and not specific, concrete stories or examples.
We hold the priesthood of all believers to be a core principle of the church.	We often empower and affirm the extra things our people do in and through the church. (We call these *sacrifices*.)
We know that we are a sent people—we say "Go in peace, serve the Lord" at the end of every service.	We judge our vitality based on how many people are drawn in to the congregation's life and activities.
We consistently proclaim the message that we are supposed to live like Jesus in the world.	We struggle to describe a Christian life as being anything more than being nice, living ethically, or volunteering for worthy causes.
We commission Sunday school teachers, stewardship visitors, council members, and mission trip participants.	We are not as intentional about blessing and supporting our roles as parents, workers, students, and citizens.
We know that people are loving, caring, and serving in their daily roles and relationships.	We persist in defining "active members" as those who attend regularly and support the congregation's work.

TRY THIS AT HOME

If you want to engage others in your congregation in a conversation on this topic, use this list as a place to start. Check the validity of the contrasting descriptions with others around you. If they ring true, talk about what it would mean to bring our intentions and practices into alignment. Which assumptions and practices are helpful and appropriate for the gathered church? What assumptions detract from the scattered church and need to be changed? What practices need to be displaced? What practices could we implement to improve our support of the scattered church? Where would job descriptions need to change to ensure that our practices support both the gathered church and the scattered church?

As an example, focus on the first pair of items in the list. Take the generic phrases of a hymn in the society, compassion, vocation, or sending sections of your hymnal and have participants write or give concrete examples of generic imperatives like "to show compassion's face" or "to speak for the broken and oppressed." Don't worry about the rhyme or meter; simply work on naming concrete examples of the commands to love and serve that we so often encounter in worship. Oh, and I don't need to tell you (do I?) that the concrete examples should come from *our lives in the world*, not congregational ministries.

Interlude: Keeping God in the Box

A pastor called the children forward for the children's sermon. She pulled out a large box containing several items, and she began, "I want you to pretend that the things in this box represent those things in my life that are important to me. As we look at these things, see if you can spot God."

The first thing she pulled out of the box was a picture of her family. She talked about who was in the picture and how important each person is to her. Then she pulled out some art supplies and talked about how much she likes to paint. Instead of pulling out a third item she asked, "Have you seen God yet?"

"No," the children replied timidly, almost questioningly.

Feigning puzzlement, she reached in and pulled out a third object, a tennis ball to represent a love of outdoor sports, then an apple to represent healthy food. "Have you seen God yet?"

"No," the children said more boldly.

Object after object came out of the box. Each time she asked the God question, the children's "No!" became louder. Finally, the last item she pulled from the bottom of the box was a cross to represent the importance of God in her life. "In all the things that we love and do," she said, "it's important to remember that God is always present, that God loves us." At long last they had found God.

The children's sermon didn't go where my imagination had taken me when it started. I imagined that the pastor was expecting the children to look for God in each of these ordinary slices of life in vain, winding up at the bottom of the box with no glimpse of God. Then the pastor would pop the surprise, saying that we hadn't been watching closely enough, because God is in every object that came out of the box. I imagined that she might read the Small Catechism's explanation of "daily bread" in the Lord's Prayer:

What then does "daily bread" mean?

Everything our bodies need, such as food, drink, clothing, shoes, house, home, fields, livestock, money, property, an upright spouse, upright children, upright workers, upright and faithful rulers, good government, good weather, peace, health, decency, honor, good friends, faithful neighbors, and the like.[1]

Then, as each object was put back in the box, she would talk about how God is providing for us and for others in all the things we do, in the activities that renew and refresh us, in the food we eat, in those who provide us with food and clothing, and in our families.

I woke up from my fantasy as the children tromped merrily away while the pastor unceremoniously dumped all those not-God objects back into the box. Yes, God went back in the box, too—the box that we too often use to limit the astonishing variety of ways that God is at work in us and through us in the everyday relationships and activities of life.

---

1. Luther, *Small Catechism*, 30.

3

Reimagining Our Roles the New Testament Way

The previous chapter pointed to perceived differences between baptized Christians and ordained leaders. The difference was at work when the pastors reported the perception that they "do ministry" and everybody else consumes it. It showed up in the comments about pastors being hired to do ministry so that everybody else can live a regular life. It can be seen in the common assumption that pastors are somehow better or more qualified to do ministry than anybody else, that they are closer to God, and that pastors don't understand what it means to deal with life in the real world.

If these assumptions are not operative, then why do we almost always call on the pastor to say the prayer at a congregational meal or meeting? Why do we assume that a pastor's visit to a hospital is somehow more effective than that of a family member or friend?[1] Why is it that I as a pastor am the one singled out to answer the drunk uncle's lifelong, unanswered question about God at a member's wedding?

How did we get to this point? Why does this difference seem to exist? Perhaps the perceived differences between pastors and their people indicate that some additional historical and theological perspective might be helpful. This chapter looks at questions like these: Where did the clergy/

---

1. See Foss, *Power Surge,* 25–27, for an insightful story of how he found himself displacing a member of their church from her rightful place at the hospital bed of a patient simply because he was the pastor who was there to perform ministry on behalf of the church.

laity tension originate? Is it normative? In what other ways might we look at this? This chapter not only belies the difference between pastors and the people, it points to the reality that ministry is entrusted to all God's people in the waters of baptism. This chapter leads to a way to talk about ministry that doesn't rely on perceived differences but on our common calling.

SO WHAT DOES THE BIBLE HAVE TO SAY ABOUT PASTORS AND LAY PEOPLE?

If we go back to the Bible will we find pastors and lay people like we heard in chapter 2? Expert providers and consumers? An elite few and unprivileged masses?

Well, if you go back to the Old Testament you *will* find something that looks a lot like that. The Old Testament does not use the word *pastor* but it does use a closely related word, *priest*. Israel's priests were intermediaries between God and God's people, bringing the concerns of the people to God and bringing God's Word or blessing to the people.

Old Testament priests were descendants of Aaron.[2] If you were a male born into that clan, you would spend your life as a priest. Priests were set apart for holy acts, for burning incense, saying prayers, offering the bulls and doves on the altar, and blowing the trumpet to remind people of God's presence. In fact, the descendants of Aaron were so thoroughly set apart that they did not receive parcels of land when the Hebrew people occupied the Promised Land, as the other eleven tribes did. While they didn't receive comfortable parsonages next to the temple, they were provided with food by the other tribes who had land and produced food. There was a definite hierarchy among the priests. Only one of Aaron's direct descendants, the high priest, could enter the Holy of Holies in the Tabernacle (and later in the Temple), once a year on the Day of Atonement.[3]

It is safe to assume that most people see a good bit of similarity between Old Testament priests and contemporary clergy. Priests were chosen to serve in the Temple, just as pastors are called to serve in the church. So, in terms of being seen as caretakers of the holy place and speaking God's

---

2. See Num 3–4, Ex 28–29, and Lev 8–9 for a sampling of how the priesthood was originally structured.

3. See Ex 27:21–28:43; 30:10; Neh 10:38; 2 Chron 13:10b; compare 1 Chron 24; Heb 9:1ff especially v. 7.

Word, there are similarities. But when we turn to the New Testament, things change dramatically.

Name a New Testament priest. Go ahead. Name a New Testament priest who comes to mind. I'll wait while you think of one . . .

Not easy, is it? While *priest* or *priests* is used ninety-five times in the gospels, with few exceptions (for example a priest named Zechariah in Luke 1 and 2 who becomes the father of John the Baptist) the priests in the gospels were not role models. Most of the time they were wholly opposed to Jesus and what he was saying and doing.

Once you move beyond the gospels, though, and the story turns to the development and struggles of the early church, the use of the word *priest* disappears almost completely . . . except in one book: Hebrews. Of the sixty-three uses of *priest* or *priests* outside of the gospels, thirty-five of those are in the book of Hebrews. When Hebrews uses the word *priest* it is talking about the "great high priest who has passed through the heavens." Do you recognize who this high priest is? It is none other than "Jesus, the Son of God" (4:14).

Remember what was just said about the role of the high priest in the Old Testament? He was the top dog, the one and only priest who got to enter the Holy of Holies. What does Hebrews say about Jesus? "He entered once for all into the Holy Place, not with the blood of goats and calves, but with his own blood, thus obtaining eternal redemption" (9:12).

> Therefore, my friends, since we have confidence to enter the sanctuary by the blood of Jesus, by the new and living way that he opened for us through the curtain (that is, through his flesh), and since we have a great priest over the house of God, let us approach with a true heart in full assurance of faith, with our hearts sprinkled clean from an evil conscience and our bodies washed with pure water. (Heb 10:19–22)

In a radical move, Jesus became both the high priest and the sacrifice. Gone forever was the need for priests to offer sacrifice to God. Jesus became the one and only mediator of God's mercy and grace. Luther affirms this observation in his treatise, "Concerning Ministry" of 1523:

> First, regard as an unmovable rock that the New Testament knows of no priest who is or can be anointed externally. If there are such, they are imitators and idols. There is neither example nor

command nor a simple word in Gospels or Epistles of the apostles in support of this vanity.[4]

Interestingly, at the same time that the role of priest (in terms of one who is in a superior position to other believers) is eliminated, the New Testament makes a second radical, even contradictory move: it also *expands* the role of priest to embrace not just one tribe or family, but the entire body of believers. *All believers* are now described as priests. "But you are a chosen race, a royal priesthood, a holy nation, God's own people, in order that you may proclaim the mighty acts of him who called you out of darkness into his marvelous light" (1 Pet. 2:9).

The above quote from Luther's treatise, "Concerning Ministry," continues:

> For a priest, especially in the New Testament, was not made but was born. He was created, not ordained. He was born not indeed of flesh, but through a birth of the Spirit, by water and Spirit in the washing of regeneration [John 3:6f.; Titus 3:5f.]. *Indeed, all Christians are priests, and all priests are Christians.*"[5]

Hold on to those two seemingly contradictory New Testament developments for a while: in the New Testament the priesthood is both eliminated *and* universalized to include all believers. We'll come back to that tension a little later in a very surprising way.

THE NEW TESTAMENT OPENS WINDOWS TO A DIFFERENT WORLD

In addition to *priest*, there are other words in the Bible that are related to our understanding of someone who is ordained. It is worth conducting a brief review of those words to see where our understandings of ministry (and who does it) differ from that of the Bible, and to look for some alternate ways of understanding and empowering ministry in the gathered and scattered church.

---

4. Luther, *LW* 40, 19.

5. Ibid., italics added.

Minister

While the Old Testament is rife with references to priests, the word *minister* is used in a similar manner, but less frequently. First Chronicles 16:4–6 describes their role:

> [David] appointed certain of the Levites as *ministers* before the ark of the Lord, to invoke, to thank, and to praise the Lord, the God of Israel. Asaph was the chief, and second to him Zechariah, Jeiel, Shemiramoth, Jehiel, Mattithiah, Eliab, Benaiah, Obed-edom, and Jeiel, with harps and lyres; Asaph was to sound the cymbals, and the priests Benaiah and Jahaziel were to blow trumpets regularly, before the ark of the covenant of God.

In the forums I conducted, it was in the definitions of *minister* that people came closest to the *mis*understanding of ministry that I had expected to find. As was reported earlier, while it was rare, people do define a minister as someone who goes into the ministry. Those who have heard a call from God and who have been seminary educated and ordained are set apart as a congregation's minister. The question that naturally arises out of this line of thinking is this: If a minister is one who is called into the ministry, what is left for the rest of God's people?

Greg Ogden points out how the New Testament runs counter to this common understanding:

> Nowhere in the New Testament does the term "ministry" or "minister" refer to a particular class of people set apart from the rest of the church. The noun *diakonia* is variously translated "service," "ministry," or "mission." The personal form of the noun *diakonos* is translated "servants," "ministers," or "deacons," depending on its context.[6]

As most of the people affirmed in the forums I conducted, ministry (that is, service or mission) in Christ's name is something that is given to all of God's people in the waters of baptism, not just a chosen few who are called to it or trained for it.

---

6. Ogden, *Unfinished Business*, 83.

Saints

When we think of saints, we think of the spiritual elite. Mother Teresa was a saint. If it can be proved that someone was party to extraordinary, other-than-human feats of healing or heroic virtues, the church recognizes her or him as a saint—someone in whom we have caught a glimpse of what God is like.

While recognition of heroic virtues is one use of the word *saint*, it's not the only way that it is used, either in the Bible or in the contemporary church. In the New Testament, the word is always a reference to all the people of God, not just the spiritual elite.[7] For example, look at Romans 1:7. Paul's letter to the Christians in Rome is addressed, "To all God's beloved in Rome, who are called to be *saints*: Grace to you and peace from God our Father and the Lord Jesus Christ." Of its sixty-two appearances in the New Testament, the word *saint* is *never used in the singular*.

In one surprising usage, Paul opens First Corinthians with the address, "To the church of God that is in Corinth, to those who are sanctified in Christ Jesus, called to be saints" (1 Cor 1:2). In large part, Paul was writing because the Corinthians had the reputation of being one of the most divisive, immoral, and troublesome of the churches Paul had visited or helped start. And yet Paul calls them *saints*.

Actually that is not surprising, for in the New Testament followers of Jesus are saints not because of our purity, piety, or miraculous deeds, but because we have been set apart by God to proclaim God's marvelous deeds. Like the New Testament uses the word, most denominations today use *saints* to describe all of God's people. Saints aren't just dead people who accomplished miraculous feats in another era. In keeping with the celebration of All Saints Day, we talk about *all* of God's saints, living and dead, who join in the witness to God's amazing love at work in the world.

Clergy

If we were to write a definition of *clergy* based on commonly held assumptions, it would probably be along the lines of "people who take care of spiritual things so everybody else can enjoy the temporal."[8] At least that's

---

7. See Ibid., 80.

8. Ibid., 89. The words in quotes here are meant to be a definition; they are a paraphrase of Ogden's sentence that inspired this definition.

what people on airplanes or at wedding receptions seem to think when the conversation gets around to what pastors do for a living. In many people's minds, both inside and outside the church, clergy are specialists in the things of God, someone that everybody else can turn to should they find themselves in need of a word from God.

The roots of the word *clergy* go back to the Greek word *klēros* (klay'-ros), which means "lot," "share," or "inheritance." It is often used to refer to the inheritance all God's people receive in Christ. Hendrik Kraemer says that the New Testament uses *klēros* to talk about the new community of men and women "who share in God's gift of redemption and glory, which is their 'inheritance' (*klēros*)."[9]

My intention is not to drag you through a Greek translation swamp to overwhelm you, but rather to point out something that is amazing and revealing. All of this points to a basic New Testament fact that is hard to ignore: We are *all* God's *klēros*, that is, we have all received the inheritance, the lot, the calling of being God's people. We are all people who share in God's work in the world. In short, we are *all* God's clergy.

Hang in there for a little longer, because the amazing part is just beginning.

Laity

Returning to common assumptions again, if you're not among the clergy, then you must be _____. It's hard to use the word clergy without also using lay, laity, or layperson. In many cases, if not most, clergy and lay are used to contrast one another. *The Oxford English Dictionary* provides a case in point: *Clergy* is defined as "The clerical order; the body of [persons] set apart by ordination for religious service in the Christian church; *opposed to laity*."[10] Likewise *laity* is defined as "The body of people not in orders, *as opposed to clergy*."[11] Ogden refers to another author who says the laity "have a strong element of 'over-againstness' toward the clergy—the clergy are, the laity are *not*, the clergy do, the laity do *not*. Nobody wants to be an is *not*."[12]

The New Testament word behind the English *laity* is *laos* (lah-os'), which means "the people of God." In stark contrast to common assumptions

---

9. Kraemer, *Theology of the Laity*, 52.

10. *OED*, Vol. III, 311, italics added.

11. *OED*, Vol. VIII, 595, italics added.

12. Ogden, *Unfinished Business*, 91.

today, *laos* is filled with dignity and honor. What started in the Old Testament as God's special people ("I will be your God and you shall be my people," Lev. 26:12) gets transferred to the New Testament understanding of the *laos* as the people of God. Ogden notes:

> *Laos* exudes a sense of specialness. . . . Out of all the peoples (*ethnos*) of the earth, there is a special people (*laos*) who are God's called-out people. The *laos* of God are nothing less than a new humanity, the vanguard of the future, the prototype of the kingdom of God not yet completed, a people of the future living in the present.[13]

When we use *laity* in a pejorative sense, we do a disservice to our baptism. Describing someone as "only a lay person" is incredibly unhelpful, unbiblical, and it is contrary to the life of faith. George Peck notes the irony of the church's dismissal of the abilities of lay people:

> Here, as in other areas of contemporary experience, we have a language problem! Frequently we are dealing with people who in their major area of activity are very competent and well trained (homemakers, farmers, miners, businesspersons, professionals of various kinds), but yet we insist on calling them, in the church, "lay people."[14]

Ogden adds, "Next time we hear someone say, 'I'm just a layperson,' we can say, 'That's more than enough.' "[15]

A SURPRISING COLLUSION

We have discovered that in the New Testament the role of priest as it was understood at the time was eliminated, and at the same time the role of priest was expanded to embrace, not just one tribe or family, but the entire body of believers. I asked you to hold on to these two seemingly contradictory thoughts for a while because we would come back to them a little later—in a very surprising way. That time has come.

If we take this biblical review as a whole, we find this surprise: all people claimed by God in the waters of baptism are all *klēros* (clergy), heirs of Christ's ministry, priests, ministers, and saints; *and* we are all *laos* (laity),

---

13. Ibid., 91–92.

14. Peck and Hoffman, *Laity in Ministry*, 16.

15. Ogden, *Unfinished Business*, 92.

the chosen people of God. It's both/and not either/or, and definitely not different from or over against each other.

What is intriguing is that when the New Testament was written there was a rich vocabulary in the Greek language to describe leaders *if* the authors had wanted to describe the power and authority assumptions that are prevalent today. In particular, there were four widely used words[16] available to the New Testament authors to describe leaders or people in places of privilege and honor, but none of these words were used to describe the ministry of early believers.[17] Instead, the accounts recorded in the New Testament follow Jesus' example: "But you are not to be called rabbi, for you have one teacher, and you are all students. And call no one your father on earth, for you have one Father—the one in heaven. Nor are you to be called instructors, for you have one instructor, the Messiah" (Matt 23:8–10).

The New Testament is clear: authority, power—ministry itself—is distributed among all of God's people, with Jesus as the head. "Truly I tell you, whatever you bind on earth will be bound in heaven, and whatever you loose on earth will be loosed in heaven. Again, truly I tell you, if two of you agree on earth about anything you ask, it will be done for you by my Father in heaven. For where two or three are gathered in my name, I am there among them" (Matthew 18:18–20). This distribution of authority shows up clearly in the verses just before the passage just quoted. Jesus gave his followers instructions on how to handle sin in the church: If someone sins against you, go to that person first. If that doesn't work, "take one or two others along with you, so that every word may be confirmed by the evidence of two or three witnesses" (18:15–16). There was to be no boss, no head honcho, and no one more qualified than others—outside of Jesus.

If the authors of the New Testament *wanted* to talk about the one person in charge of all the rest, then one of the four Greek words mentioned earlier for leader, ruler, or office holder would have been used. Instead, and very surprisingly, the dominant word in the New Testament to describe this broad-based ministry was a word that was rarely used in other writings of the time: *diakonia* (dee-ak-on-ee'-ah), *service*, especially that of serving at a table. Even the personal form of the word, *diakonos* (dee-ak'-oh-nos; servant, slave, waiter) was not in wide use. In restaurants today it is common

---

16. *timē*—honor; *archē* or *archas*—ruler, leader, the first among many; *leitourgia*—public ministry, service; and *telos*—usually associated with "the end," it can also mean the highest government office, or magistrate.

17. Schweizer, "*Ministry in the Early Church*," 835–41.

to call such a person a *server*. It's curious that a secular, domestic term would be chosen to describe ministry in the church when there were other perfectly good, widely understood words for people who are charged with leadership.

> This spontaneous usage [of servant language] in all the different layers of the NT literature shows what an impression the challenge of Jesus' way of life and teaching made on all his followers. The total (eschatological) newness of a service without institutional hierarchies or resort to force was so striking that it became impossible to speak of the honor or the exemplary model of an "official" ministry apart from that of any other person in the church. Wherever somebody was serving Christ, it was exactly what a slave would do for his lord, i.e., a simple, worldly service, not a domination of others.[18]

Indeed, in the early church, it was as Jesus said it should be: "The greatest among you will be your servant. All who exalt themselves will be humbled, and all who humble themselves will be exalted" (Matt 23:11–12). The New Testament clearly describes and lifts up "the whole people of God" for whom the head is Christ. There is no comparison or contrasting of roles, there are no gifts missing in that body, and there is no hierarchy of ministries.

In fact, it sounds a lot like what Peter said was spoken through the prophet Joel:

> In the last days it will be, God declares,
> that I will pour out my Spirit upon all flesh,
> and your sons and your daughters shall prophesy,
> and your young men shall see visions,
> and your old men shall dream dreams.
> Even upon my slaves, both men and women,
> in those days I will pour out my Spirit;
> and they shall prophesy. (Acts 2:17–18)

If this is the way it was in the early church, even the way Jesus intended it to be, perhaps we should invoke the wedding line, What God has joined together . . .

---

18. Ibid., 836.

THE SHAPE OF LEADERSHIP IN THE NEW TESTAMENT

By this time (if not well before) some readers are probably thinking, *But the New Testament does talk about presbyters, elders, bishops, evangelists and the like!* That is a relevant observation, and it is something that we cannot overlook. At the same time that the New Testament establishes the priesthood of the whole people of God under the leadership of Jesus, it also makes references to various roles among the people. But as we will see below, the definition of these roles is fluid and equating them to roles in the current church is challenging.

Yes, there are people in the New Testament's account of the early church who have distinct roles and tasks, but clergy and lay were not the distinct categories that we know today. When the New Testament mentions leaders, they are cast in a wide variety of roles, with a wide variety of titles. It's difficult to say exactly what each of the roles and titles means, partly because they are sometimes used interchangeably, and sometimes we're hindered by the vagaries of translation. Nevertheless, a brief review of the various terms used in the New Testament is revealing.

Apostle(s) is used over forty times outside of the gospels, but it usually refers to the original twelve or to Paul (who claims his own apostleship, even though he never met Jesus in the flesh). Barnabas and a few others are called apostles but that's fairly rare. First Corinthians 12:28 mentions apostles in a more generic form ("And God has appointed in the church first apostles, second prophets, third teachers . . . ") as does Ephesians 4:11, "The gifts he gave were that some would be apostles, some prophets, some evangelists, some pastors and teachers . . . " For the most part, though, the use of *apostle(s)* is limited to a fairly select group, rather than being used to describe leaders throughout the early church.

Diakonos is probably the most widely used term to describe leaders. Depending on the context, *diakonos* is translated as deacon, servant, helper, or minister. Variants are used at least twenty-five times outside of the gospels, and they are clearly a reflection of Jesus' emphasis on servanthood.

Prophets is the next most frequently used term. Searching for the words *prophet(s), prophesy,* and *prophecy* yields about twenty-four verses outside of the gospels (excluding verses that clearly refer to Old Testament counterparts). A number of prophets are named, and women are included in this category. One of the more interesting passages that shows the vitality of prophecy in the early church is 1 Corinthians 14:29. In a description of public worship Paul says, "Let two or three prophets speak, and let the others weigh what is said."

Elder is a common term, too, as it is used about twenty times. It's difficult to nail down exactly who and what an elder was. In some cases it seems to be a second-generation witness: apostles (at least the twelve) knew Jesus and elders knew the apostles. It is interesting that in Acts 15 and 16 "apostles and elders" are always mentioned as one, or at least together. In other places, though, this might simply be a term for older and wiser members of the church. In at least one case (Acts 14:23) there is mention of elders being appointed, which could imply some sort of intentional role in the community.

Teachers (or *teaching*) are mentioned a dozen times. Interestingly, teachers are often paired with prophets. And in Ephesians 4:11 the Greek behind "pastors and teachers" could also be translated "teaching pastor" (or more accurately, in keeping with the next paragraph, "teaching shepherd").

Shepherd/Pastor is used eight times outside of the gospels. The same word that is used in the gospels to describe shepherds keeping watch o'er their flocks by night is used in the early church to talk about leaders. In most cases, the Greek is translated into English as *shepherd*. In Ephesians 4:11, though, many translations (though not all) translate the Greek as *pastor*. One definition of *pastor* is, "a shepherd of souls; one who has the spiritual oversight over a company or body of Christians, as bishop, priest, minister, etc.,"[19] so the words can be used somewhat interchangeably. It is worth noting that *pastor* is used only once (in Ephesians 4:11), and that is only if you choose to translate the Greek that way instead of *shepherd*.

Bishop/Overseer is used infrequently. The Greek word behind the English translation literally means someone who has oversight over someone or something. Now is as good a time as any to mention that *elder/presbyter*, *shepherd/pastor*, and *overseer/bishop* can be and are used interchangeably, as in 1 Peter 5:1-2, "Now as an elder myself and a witness of the sufferings of Christ, as well as one who shares in the glory to be revealed, I exhort the *elders* among you to tend [literally, *shepherd*] the flock of God that is in your charge, exercising the *oversight*, not under compulsion but willingly, as God would have you do it—not for sordid gain but eagerly."

Leader/Manager are words that represent a few Greek words translated in the New Testament as *leader*, *manager*, *charge*, or *rule*. I only found

19. *OED*, Vol. XI, 323.

five verses that use these words, and two of those refer to managing one's household affairs well.

Evangelists round out this review of leadership positions. The definition of the Greek word is "preacher of the gospel: evangelist." We could just as easily translate the three passages that use this word with the modern term *preacher*.

(If you would like to explore these roles in more detail, check out the list of verses in which these roles are found at www.TheScattering.org.)

It is worth noting that when the New Testament mentions these roles, in nearly all cases, they are referred to in the plural, which seems to indicate that there were several prophets or many elders in any given place. While Timothy in Ephesus and Titus in Crete are named in the singular, there is no example or direction in Scripture that dictates or supports only one such leader in any given congregation. Instead we find repeated references to a wide variety of leaders, roles, and functions (not to mention names). In addition, as we have seen, sometimes the words used to describe the roles seem to be interchangeable.

Consider this passage:

> To each is given the manifestation of the Spirit for the common good. To one is given through the Spirit the utterance of wisdom, and to another the utterance of knowledge according to the same Spirit, to another faith by the same Spirit, to another gifts of healing by the one Spirit, to another the working of miracles, to another prophecy, to another the discernment of spirits, to another various kinds of tongues, to another the interpretation of tongues. All these are activated by one and the same Spirit, who allots to each one individually just as the Spirit chooses.
>
> For just as the body is one and has many members, and all the members of the body, though many, are one body, so it is with Christ. For in the one Spirit we were all baptized into one body— Jews or Greeks, slaves or free—and we were all made to drink of one Spirit. . . .
>
> Now you are the body of Christ and individually members of it. And God has appointed in the church first apostles, second prophets, third teachers; then deeds of power, then gifts of healing, forms of assistance, forms of leadership, various kinds of tongues. Are all apostles? Are all prophets? Are all teachers? Do all work miracles? Do all possess gifts of healing? Do all speak in tongues? Do all interpret? But strive for the greater gifts. And I will show you a still more excellent way. (1 Cor 12:7–13, 27–31)

Where is the solo pastor in that passage? Where is the ordained leader?[20] There simply is none. "To each is given the manifestation of the Spirit for the common good." The people of God, together, make up the body, under the leadership of Jesus. A little later Paul makes this even clearer:

> When you come together, each one has a hymn, a lesson, a revelation, a tongue, or an interpretation. Let all things be done for building up. If anyone speaks in a tongue, let there be only two or at most three, and each in turn; and let one interpret. But if there is no one to interpret, let them be silent in church and speak to themselves and to God. Let two or three prophets speak, and let the others weigh what is said. If a revelation is made to someone else sitting nearby, let the first person be silent. For you can all prophesy one by one, so that all may learn and all be encouraged. And the spirits of prophets are subject to the prophets, for God is a God not of disorder but of peace. (1 Cor 14:26b-33)

To be fair to the New Testament accounts, there was recognition of and support for those who assumed the various leadership roles mentioned above. In what is probably one of the earliest letters in the New Testament (a dozen or so years after the resurrection) Paul very clearly says, "[W]e appeal to you, brothers and sisters, to respect those who labor among you, and have charge of you in the Lord and admonish you; esteem them very highly in love because of their work" (1 Thess 5:12–13a).

Later, Paul writes:

> Now, brothers and sisters, you know that members of the household of Stephanas were the first converts in Achaia, and they have devoted themselves to the service of the saints; I urge you to put yourselves at the service of such people, and of everyone who works and toils with them. I rejoice at the coming of Stephanas and Fortunatus and Achaicus, because they have made up for your absence; for they refreshed my spirit as well as yours. So give recognition to such persons. (1 Cor 16:15–18)

---

20. There is one verse in the New Testament (NRSV) that uses the word "ordain," 1 Timothy 5:22. It comes toward the end of a paragraph that talks about elders—bad elders in particular—and it says "Do not ordain anyone hastily." The Greek behind this phrase is more accurately "Lay hands on no one hastily." While the laying on of hands is one part of an ordination service today, it might be that the translators of the NRSV were a little too anxious to show our modern equivalent at work in the New Testament. Many other translations use the phrase, "lay on hands," which appears to be a way of recognizing leaders in the early church.

Clearly there were leaders in the early church, but the roles were fluid, and most importantly they were spread out across the Body of Christ. The New Testament simply doesn't describe the reality that we live with. The hierarchy and class distinctions that are pervasive in the Old Testament were eliminated, and the New Testament does not anticipate the restoration of the hierarchy and class distinction that we know.[21] Instead, it spread the work of ministry across the breadth and depth of the whole people of God.

> [I]n Christ the people *as a whole* become the servant of the Lord. Baptism is the universal ordination of people into the universal ministry of the people of God . . . Leaders are merely people who serve other servants in a particular way.[22]

SO WHERE, WHEN, AND HOW DID THINGS CHANGE?

One question, then, emerges: How was the New Testament's radical and egalitarian revolution undone?

While the church was still in its infancy, in the second half of the first century and the first half of the second century, a group of five men known now as the Apostolic Fathers had great influence. It is important to note that many books in the New Testament were still being penned while the Apostolic Fathers were alive, and they too were writing influential letters and books. While many of their writings still exist, none of them were included in the New Testament when it was finalized several centuries later. Had some of their writings been included in the New Testament, the foregoing section about leaders in the New Testament would have to be rewritten. In particular, one Apostolic Father, Ignatius, described church leaders called *bishops*. "Be obedient to the bishop and to one another, as Jesus Christ was to the Father [according to the flesh], and as the Apostles were to Christ and to the Father, that there may be union both of flesh and of spirit" (Epistle of Ignatius to the Magnesians 13:2).

It would be unrealistic to assume that any group, even a group of faithful believers, could continue to exist over a long period and through

---

21. See Bosch, *Transforming Mission*, 467–74. On pg. 468 he notes, "The [early] church has offices—if we wish to call them that—particularly those of *episkopos, presbyteros,* and *diakonos* (all of them secular terms). But, first, these offices are always understood as existing within the community of faith, as never being prior to, independent of, or above the local church."

22. Stevens, *Other Six Days*, 138. Emphasis in original.

rapid growth without some form of organization or leadership. In the early centuries there were also significant differences of opinion and multiple theological interpretations on many important matters. In response to the threat of division, leaders arose in the early church. Some of these leaders were influential writers and teachers who gathered followers and made judgment calls that branded some followers as orthodox and others as heretics.[23]

David Bosch notes that by the last couple of decades of the first century,

> The church now had to cope with heresy from without and a hollowing-out of faith from within. In these circumstances the most reliable antidote appeared to have been to encourage believers to follow the directives of the clergy, in particular the bishops, who soon . . . were regarded as the sole guarantors of the apostolic tradition and the ones endowed with full authority in matters ecclesiastical.[24]

It wasn't until the fourth century, though, during the time of the Roman Emperor Constantine, that the division between clergy and lay became clearly defined.[25] Up until this time, Christianity had been mostly an underground movement that was regularly persecuted. Constantine converted to Christianity and then declared Christianity to be the official religion of the empire. Naturally, when you have an official religion, you need a structure. And what better or more successful structure was there to model this new religion after than the Roman Empire? With that, a model for ministry that looks very similar to the Old Testament priesthood, with its hierarchy and class distinctions, was back.

The sixteenth century Reformers made a valiant attempt to reinstate the biblical understanding of ministry. Luther in particular railed against the hierarchy of the church of his time. Luther called for the eradication of clerical privilege, and the concept of the universal priesthood harkened back to the New Testament understanding that all believers are both *klēros*

---

23. See Cox, *Future of Faith*, (especially the first five chapters) for a very readable and insightful look into this period of transition. Cox looks at the multifaceted nature of the early church, then traces its development into a hierarchical structure that mimicked the Roman Empire (the very opponent that the early church believed would soon be undone by the Kingdom of God).

24. Bosch, *Transforming Mission*, 468.

25. Ibid. Bosch notes, "Apart from a questionable reference in Ignatius, the term 'priest' was not applied to Christian clergy until around the year 200."

and *laos*, that all of us are called to be God's ministers (*diakonos*, servants) at work in the world.

"And yet," Kraemer says of the long-term effects of the Reformation, "it must be frankly stated that neither this new conception of the Church nor this strong vindication of the laity has ever become dominant."[26] Bosch notes,

> It is true that Luther is to be credited with the rediscovery of the notion of the "priesthood of all believers" . . . However, when Luther's understanding of church and theology was under assault from Anabaptists (some of whom had jettisoned the idea of an ordained ministry altogether) and Catholics alike, he reverted to the inherited paradigm. In the end, he still had the clergyman at the center of his church, endowed with considerable authority.[27]

Not long after Luther's time the English poet John Milton (1608–1674) wrote a very interesting critique of the church of his time. In Book 2, Chapter 3 of *The Reason of Church Government* he writes:

> This all Christians ought to know, that the title of Clergy St. Peter gave to all Gods people, till Pope Hyginus[28] and the succeeding Prelates took it from them, appropriating that name to themselves and their Priests only; and condemning the rest of Gods inheritance to an injurious and alienat condition of Laity, they separated from them by local partitions in Churches, through their grosse ignorance and pride imitating the old temple: and excluded the members of Christ from the property of being members, the bearing of orderly and fit offices in the ecclesiastical body, as if they had meant to sow up that Jewish vail which Christ by his death on the Crosse rent in sunder.

BACK TO WHERE WE STARTED

With that we find ourselves pretty much back where we started. The distinction between clergy and lay is firmly in place, and while the potential for

---

26. Kraemer. *Theology of the Laity*, 62–63.

27. Bosch, *Transforming Mission*, 469.

28. Pope Hyginus (died c. 142 CE) is traditionally credited with being the first Christian prelate to devise ranks and orders for Christian clergy, though modern scholars tend to doubt this claim and view the governance of the church of Rome during this period as still more or less collective.

the priesthood of all believers is on our lips, it has not often found its way into the life and practice of the church, other than as a generally-held truth. And yet its promise will not let us go.

One more story from the Equipping Pastors conversations comes to mind. Actually, this story didn't become apparent until I wrote this chapter and found myself looking back on the conversations and thinking, *So that's what was happening!*

In the first round of conversations with the pastors we spent a good bit of time unpacking Ephesians 4:11–12. When I started this journey, this was what I considered the go-to verse for this topic. "The gifts he gave were that some would be apostles, some prophets, some evangelists, some pastors and teachers, to equip the saints for the work of ministry." Up to that point the passage is clear and definitive: Pastors exist to equip the saints (the people) for the work of ministry.

What I didn't anticipate when I chose to focus on that passage was the rest of the sentence. The author of Ephesians continues: " . . . some pastors and teachers, to equip the saints for the work of ministry, for building up the body of Christ, until all of us come to the unity of the faith and of the knowledge of the Son of God, to maturity, to the measure of the full stature of Christ" (Eph 4:12–13).

When we studied this passage in the small group conversations among pastors, I provided a variety of translations. With Bibles in hand we were confronted with the whole passage and I was lost, as were many of the participants. We never stopped to consider the relevance of the other roles (apostles, prophets, and evangelists) mentioned in the first part of the verse, which says a lot in itself. We did, though, wonder what the follow-up phrases meant: Is "the work of ministry" a matter of "building up the body of Christ"? Did I mistakenly assume that this is a passage about ministry in the world? Is this describing nothing more than a gathered church activity after all?

What I see now is that we were simply unable to step out of our clergy v. laity roles. Apostles, prophets, and evangelists belong to another age. In our day there are pastors and there are lay people. It's the pastors' job to equip the laity. That's what the author of Ephesians is talking about, right? Given those assumptions, we were unable to make much sense out of the phrases that followed.

With the revelations of this chapter in hand it is now possible to see this entire sentence in a whole new light. The author of Ephesians was writing from a time in which there were a wide variety of roles, and those roles were meant to "build up the body," until all of us "come to the unity of the faith and of the knowledge of the Son of God, to maturity, to the measure of the full stature of Christ." That is, until we—all—become Christ's people, ministering (*diakonia*, serving) with whatever gifts God has given us, in the many arenas of our lives—inside the church to be sure, but in the world as well, perhaps even more so. When writing about Ephesians 4 Ogden says,

> The saints (Paul's designation of all God's people) are to do the work of ministry with the empowerment of apostles, prophets, evangelists, and pastor-teachers. The role of these gifted ones . . . is to bring the ministry of the whole body to its fullness, not to guard the ministry for themselves. Far from ministry being associated with a few, it is coterminous with the entire body. There is only one ministry—the ministry of the people of God.[29]

Far from being a passage simply about gathered ministries *or* scattered ministries, Ephesians 4 is about both—an organic reality. God calls us and makes us "a royal priesthood" (1 Peter 2:9), the body of Christ resurrected in our own time. We become the Body of Christ, not for our own sake, but for the world's. As Christ came to serve, so do we serve.

Near the end of a workbook that grew out of the Andover Newton Laity Project, the authors summarize what we have found thus far: "Christ's ministry is one, carried on in many ways, utilizing a variety of gifts. We need to reclaim a vision of laity and clergy in ministry as an interdependent whole."[30]

R. Paul Stevens put it this way:

> All are clergy in the sense of being appointed by God to service and dignified as God's inheritance. All have a share in the power and blessing of the age of the Spirit. All are laity in the sense of having their identity rooted in the people of God. All give ministry. All receive ministry. That is the constitution of the church.[31]

This isn't a matter of one part of the Body of Christ doing something for another part. This is about being the Body, in its wholeness, "until all of

---

29. Ogden, *Unfinished Business*, 85.

30. Broholm, and Hoffman, "Empowering Laity." The sections are not numbered, and the page numbers begin at "1" with each new section, which makes specific page references impossible. This quote is from the first page of the essay, "Content of Ministry." See Peck and Hoffman, *Laity in Ministry* for more on this project.

31. Stevens, *Other Six Days*, 39.

us come to the unity of the faith and of the knowledge of the Son of God, to maturity, to the measure of the full stature of Christ." . . . until we all become like Christ. . . . until we all *become* Christ at work: loving, caring, serving, healing, feeding, comforting, and restoring broken people and a broken world.

Stepping out of our lay v. clergy roles is the first step toward imagining a church that connects faith and life. As Ogden said, "There is only one ministry—the ministry of the people of God," and it was given to us in the waters of baptism. Seeing ministry as something that is entrusted to *all* of God's people is critical. When we do that, the priesthood of all believers will not only be on our lips; it will finally find its way into the life and practice of the church.

4

Building on the Imagination
of Predecessors

You can't know where you are going
until you know where you've come from.

The book of Genesis tells us that God created everything that exists out of nothing. While God is capable of creating something out of nothing, that is not true of us. When we set out to work on something, we might think that we are blazing new trails, but most of the time we're not. We are the product a long line of ancestors. Our interests and passions arise out of experiences and education. One scientific experiment usually proceeds from another. Likewise, our beliefs and practices are passed on to us from those who have gone before us.

Most of the time that which we have inherited from the saints who have gone before us is valuable and we want to hold on to it. This chapter lifts up vocation as one part of our inheritance that we certainly want to keep. We will look at the concept of vocation over time: from the Bible, through the early church, the Reformation, and in our day. As the story unfolds you will understand how frequently this topic has come up, not just in our day, but through the centuries. At the same time, as we look at this history, you will discover that we have so consistently focused on the work of the gathered church that we have overlooked the premise and the promise of an essential characteristic of the church: equipping the saints for their ministry in the world.

CALLED FROM THE START

As we saw in chapter 1, the answer to our questions about meaning and purpose show up at the very beginning of the biblical story.

> God said, "Let us make humankind in our image, according to our likeness; and let them have dominion over the fish of the sea, and over the birds of the air, and over the cattle, and over all the wild animals of the earth, and over every creeping thing that creeps upon the earth."
> So God created humankind in his image,
> in the image of God he created them;
> male and female he created them. (Genesis 1:26–27)[1]

As it has been since the beginning of time, God continues the work of creation—and Genesis reminds us that God's continuing work of creation and caring for creation is done *through us*. We are not just recipients of all that God has done and continues to do; we are meant to be participants, co-creators with God, and (as we saw in chapter 1) in that we find clues to our purpose.

The Bible is clear: God expects that in whatever we do, wherever we do it, and with whomever we are connected, we will bear witness to God's love for all people and all creation. Certainly this work to which we are called happens in and through the gathered church, but by no means does it stop there. We are meant to bear God's image in *all of life*, when we are gathered *and* when we are scattered.

---

1. Likewise, see the second creation story in Genesis 2:19 "So out of the ground the Lord God formed every animal of the field and every bird of the air, and brought them to the man to see what he would call them; and whatever the man called every living creature, that was its name." A seemingly inconsequential act for us (we let our kids name the family pets, after all), this was considered an act of great power in ancient Hebrew circles. If you knew someone's name that meant you had power over him or her. (That's why to this day many Jews will not utter the name Yahweh for fear that God would perceive that they are attempting to control the uncontrollable One.) If you had the ability to name someone or something, that was a sign of even greater power. In short, like Genesis 1, in Genesis 2 humans are given power over creation.

THE COMMUNITY OF THE CALLED

Biblical passages that call us to love our neighbors as ourselves resulted in an interesting name for the community that gathers and is sent in God's name. We need to look at a few ancient words in order to show how thoroughly the biblical call to love our neighbor is embedded in our spiritual DNA.

The New Testament word for "calling" or "to be called" is the Greek word *klésis* (clay-sis). What is interesting about this word is that a similar Greek word is used for the church—*ekklésia* (ek-clay-see'-ah). Take a good look at the Greek word for calling, and compare it to the Greek word for church. Do you see it? If you break *ekklésia* down to its roots, you have *ek* and *klésia*. The first half, *ek*, is the Greek word for "out"; *klésia* comes from *klésis*, or "calling." When we put those two together and turn them around to fit English grammar we get "called out." So the New Testament's word for *church*, *ekklésia*, is a description of our purpose and character. We are a community of people who are called out, by God, for a special purpose: to love and serve the world.[2]

It's important to note here that when God calls us to do something, it is for the good of our neighbor; in Jesus' words, we are summoned to service, not to greatness. "Jesus called [the disciples] to him and said, 'You know that the rulers of the Gentiles lord it over them, and their great ones are tyrants over them. It will not be so among you; but whoever wishes to be great among you must be your servant, and whoever wishes to be first among you must be your slave; just as the Son of Man came not to be served but to serve, and to give his life a ransom for many" (Matthew 20:25–27). More importantly, considering that the culture in which we live is driven by individualism, I would add that we are called to sacrifice, not to self-fulfillment.[3]

While we're mucking around in ancient languages, let's follow the path of *calling* from the Greek to Latin. When the church came to be identified with the Holy Roman Empire in the fourth century, Latin became the dominant language of the faith, thus necessitating a translation of the Bible. The Greek word for calling (*klésis*) was translated with the Latin *vocatio* (vo-cot'-zee-oh). I trust you see where this is going. *Vocatio* is the

---

2. Give yourself bonus points if you noticed that the word *ekklésia* sounds familiar. It's the root of our word "ecclesiastical," which is defined as "of or relating to the Christian Church."

3. See Schuurman, *Discerning Our Callings*, 18; and Bennethum, *Listen!*, 42.

root for the English word *vocation*. This, then, is the beginning of story of how the biblical understanding of *calling* has survived over the centuries and through many translations. It's simply something we cannot escape. If we are Christians, we are called, not to greatness, nor to self-fulfillment, but to Christ-like, sacrificial service on behalf of our neighbor. This is our vocation.

INTO THE REFORMATION

The biblical concept of calling, or vocation as we now know it in this historical survey, was not lost on the reformers of the sixteenth century. Indeed, vocation was central to both Luther's and Calvin's understanding of what it means to be a Christian.

Luther's work on vocation was prompted by what he saw as an error of the Roman Catholic Church of his time. Over the centuries, being a faithful Christian came to be identified more and more with those who dedicated their lives to serving in and through the church: priests, nuns, monks, and popes. Luther himself entered a monastery; his own journey had been one of following the church's directions for pleasing God.[4] If you are serious about your faith, he was told, become a monk. And so he did, largely to overcome deep personal anxiety about whether he would ever be worthy of God's love. In the course of his awakening to what he called the abuses of the church of his time, Luther came to the point of objecting in the strongest of terms to the assertion that one could ever earn God's love through religious devotion.

In his essay *On Monastic Vows*, Luther attacked the understanding that there is one way, a better way, to serve God. In his classic story of Luther's life, Roland Bainton sums up Luther's writing on religious vows as a way to please God: "Monastic vows rest on the false assumption that there is a special calling, *a vocation*, to which superior Christians are invited to observe the counsels of perfection while ordinary Christians fulfill only the commands; but there simply is no special religious vocation, declared Luther, since the call of God comes to each man at the common tasks."[5]

---

4. Read the first few chapters of Bainton, *Here I Stand,* for a very helpful telling of Luther's journey from doubt to grace.

5. Bainton, *Here I Stand*, 156. Emphasis in original.

Later in *On Monastic Vows* Luther says (in his typically bombastic way) that vows to become a monk and thereby to withdraw from life in the world are sinful. Wingren explains:

> Luther shows monastic vows to be contrary to faith, to freedom, to God's command and love, and to reason. A monastic vow is accordingly a vow to do evil. [The vow] must be broken, even as a vow to steal, to lie, or to murder. [quoting Luther] "It ought not to be argued whether you vow with good or evil intent, when it is certain that what you vowed was bad. One ought to be faithful to the gospel; and such vows, for whatever cause they were made, with whatever intention, and at whatever time, ought to be forsaken with all confidence, and subjected to the liberty of Christian faith."[6]

If that wasn't blunt enough language, Wingren elaborates, "Luther goes the whole way, and declares that the orders of pope, bishop, priest, and monk, 'as they are now,' are sinful orders like robbery, usury, and prostitution."[7] In order to understand this harsh criticism, remember what we found in chapter 1: For Luther, faith (and faith alone) is directed toward God; acts of devotion and love, on the other hand, are directed toward our neighbors, not so that we can earn God's favor, but that they might have what they need to live. In this case, the error that upset Luther was that the church was teaching that religious vows could earn favor with God rather than directing followers to engage in works for one's neighbor. Paraphrasing a passage from Luther's Christmas sermon on John 21:19–24, Wingren writes, "Just orders, such as are ordained by God or those whose existence is not contrary to God's will, are husbands and wives, boys and girls, lords and ladies, governors, regents, judges, officeholders, farmers, citizens, etc."[8] In other places Luther reasserts this view: vocation is not the pursuit of religious superheroes, but it is a common calling that all people receive. You don't need religious garb in order to live out God's love; indeed, doctors in

---

6. Wingren, *Luther on Vocation*, 2. Wingren cites *WA* 8 668; see pg. 664 for the Luther quote.

7. Ibid., 3.

8. Ibid., 3. The paraphrased sentence in *Luther's Works* reads, "And when I talk about calling [German: *Stand*] which is not sinful in itself, I don't mean thereby that anyone can live here on earth without sin (all callings and estates sin daily), rather I mean the callings that God has set—or that are not established against God—such as: legitimate laborer, maid, husband, wife, overlord, judge, office holder, farmer, citizen, and so on." *WA* 10 I, 1, 317. Kathryn Kleinhans provided this translation at my request.

lab coats, farmers in overalls, and bakers in aprons are God's instruments of love as much as clerics in fancy robes.

This finds its expression in the most basic of all the teachings of the Reformation. The Small Catechism is a short, simple, and memorizable explanation of the faith that parents were expected to teach to their children. In the section on the Lord's Prayer and its request, "Give us today our daily bread," Luther asks, "What then does 'daily bread' mean?" The catechism answers, "Everything our bodies need, such as food, drink, clothing, shoes, house, home, fields, livestock, money, property, an upright spouse, upright children, upright workers, upright and faithful rulers, good government, good weather, peace, health, decency, honor, good friends, faithful neighbors, and the like." Indeed, Luther explains in the prior paragraph, "God gives daily bread without our asking, even to all evil people."[9] God does this, not through miraculous intervention like manna falling from the sky, but by way of farmers who plant and harvest the grain, bakers who turn flour into bread, warehouse workers and wholesale distributors, truck drivers, shelf stockers, and clerks at the checkout counter. Oh, and lest we forget, other people play roles as well: bankers, agricultural scientists, advertisers, lawyers, and food safety inspectors.

We could go on to name more people who play a role in bringing bread to our table, but we need to look back at the Small Catechism's list one more time. So far, we've only considered people involved in providing our daily *bread*. What if we listed everyone who is involved in bringing us all the types of food we consume? What about the parallels to bread that the Small Catechism lists? We could fill the rest of this book with examples of vocations (serving the neighbor's needs) if we included people who bring us "clothing, shoes, house, home, fields, livestock, money, property, an upright spouse, upright children, upright workers, upright and faithful rulers, good government, good weather, peace, health, decency, honor, good friends, faithful neighbors, and the like." To circle back to where this chapter began, this endless list reminds us that God continues the work of creation *through us*, ordinary people in the roles, relationships, and responsibilities of our ordinary lives.

---

9. Luther, *Small Catechism*, 30.

IN OUR DAY

As I pondered Luther's list of the means by which God provides our daily bread (it didn't take nearly as many people to get bread on the table in Luther's day as it does in ours!), I was struck by how quaint Luther's explanation seemed. At the very least, the list of people involved in Luther's day would have been much more personal than it is in our day. (One would buy his or her bread from the neighborhood baker, which would eliminate current day advertisers, warehouse workers, truck drivers, as well as many others.) But that in no way means that Luther's assertion that God is at work in and through us to provide for our neighbors' needs has been eliminated by our advanced food production, warehousing, and marketing. If anything, the list of people we depend on for our daily bread (and our food and clothing, home and property, orderly community, etc.) has expanded dramatically over the past five centuries.

The Reformation-era concept of vocation sought to tie our faith to our work (and to our relationships, civic and familial responsibilities, and other non-compensated roles). The longing to strengthen the connection of faith and work has not gone away. In fact, in recent decades a wide variety of people have sought to strengthen it.

A few years ago, when my interest in this subject was rekindled, one of the early surprises I encountered was how many people have advocated for a connection between faith and work. I was also surprised to find out that it had been a topic of conversation (not to mention publishing) for more years than I had ever considered. A note that I wrote about one of the first books I read on this leg of my journey was, "This book pays for itself with the footnote that is embedded in the opening sentences. Footnote 2 lists books printed from 1952 through 1987 (shortly before this book was published) that provided key turning points for the authors." The list of books in the footnote was almost half a page long.[10] My next note added that over twenty-five years had passed since the authors wrote this, during which hundreds of additional books have been published.

As I did more research, I found that the list of books in that footnote did not go back far enough. A pronouncement from the Assembly of the World Council of Churches at Amsterdam in 1948 sounds remarkably current:

---

10. Stevens and Collins, *Equipping Pastor*, 159.

Only by the witness of a spiritually intelligent and active laity can the Church meet the modern world in its actual perplexities and life situations. Since one of the hard facts of the present time is that millions of people think of the Church as floating above the modern world and entirely out of touch with it, the importance of this simple pronouncement cannot easily be over-estimated.[11]

In *God at Work: The History and Promise of the Faith at Work Movement*, David Miller traces the history of what he calls the Faith at Work movement (FAW). In the introduction he says that, contrary to the advice given in recent decades that religion and business don't mix, "growing numbers of businesspeople of all levels are attending conferences and management seminars on spirituality and work, participating in small prayer and study groups on faith and leadership, and reading books, magazines, and newsletters for self-help as regards integrating biblical teachings with marketplace demands."[12]

More to the point of our historical review of the concept of vocation, Miller's book describes three phases of the Faith At Work movement in great detail. Near the beginning of chapter 2 Miller says, "Foundational to an analysis of the current Faith at Work movement is the understanding that it is not completely new."[13] As evidence of that, he begins his survey with the *Social Gospel era* (c. 1890–1945). This movement applied Christian ethics to social problems, especially issues of social justice such as economic inequality, poverty, crime, racial tensions, and child labor, though its particular focus varied among evangelicals and liberals. The Social Gospel era also popularized special purpose groups, including Alcoholics Anonymous, Faith and Work Inc., and the Christian Business Men's Committee.[14]

The *Ministry of the Laity era* (1946–1980) begins at the same time that the World Council of Churches was addressing this topic (see above), and its end corresponds roughly with what some scholars call the sidelining of both the Protestant mainline and the World Council of Churches. I grew up and attended seminary when there was talk about "the ministry of the laity." I began my parish ministry, though, as people were backing away from that term, largely because it had suffered from mission creep, and it

---

11. *Evanston Speaks*, 104.

12. Miller, *God at Work*, 3.

13. Ibid., 23.

14. Ibid., 30–34.

had come to mean little more than support functions that the laity perform in and for the gathered church.

The *Faith at Work era* (1980-present) is Miller's terminology and, as yet, not in wide usage. The wide variety of groups associated with the Faith at Work era shows that the desire to connect one's faith with work continues. Miller uses information from Gallup polls that show an increasing desire among Americans to integrate a sense of faith or spirituality into their everyday lives. In particular, Gallup says, "Two of the underlying desires of the American people at this time are to find deeper meaning in life and to build deeper, more trusting relations with other people in our often impersonal and fragmented society."[15] The result of this desire, Miller maintains, is an increase in participation in FAW groups. He cites as his evidence for this increasing participation "surveys and studies that reveal a consistent pattern" and "informal and anecdotal evidence . . . from a review of the media, the business academy, the growth in 'spirituality and work' nonprofit organizations, personal stories of businesspeople, and conferences, newsletters and Web sites all dedicated to faith at work."[16] It is very revealing that Miller's evidence comes from secular sources:

> Notably, it is primarily the secular general and business presses that are reporting on the movement, and not the religious presses. . . . Moreover, the majority of these stories are in the business or general interest sections of the newspaper, and not in the religion section. . . . One thing that is notable about all of these stories . . . is that they are written with a respectful and generally approving tone.[17]

Miller's book was published in 2007. If he were to update the book, it is possible that he would either rename this third era or include recent efforts that are now called *spiritual leadership*.[18] Numerous books have been published, articles posted, groups formed, and conferences held on

---

15. Gallup, and Lindsay, *Surveying the Religious Landscape*, 8, as quoted in Miller, *God at Work*, 73.

16. Miller, *God at Work*, 75.

17. Ibid., 107–8

18. Miller does report trends closely related to the newer version of the topic that I'm reporting. On pp. 109–11 he lists a variety of books that have been published by businesspeople on topics like "God is my CEO" and "spirituality at work," but he never directly mentions the topic of spiritual leadership that is becoming increasingly pervasive, not to mention amorphous.

this topic.[19] This most recent expression of the FAW era is diverse, ranging from explicit faith language to simply talking about types of leadership that are not rooted in or seek a blatant profit motive.

Regardless of how one might name or distinguish eras and movements, it is sufficient to say that the work of the scattered church is a topic that simply won't go away. Strangely, though (as indicated by the secular sources Miller quotes), the scattered church has had an incredibly hard time competing with our focus on the gathered church. Which brings up the question, Why?

THE AUTOIMMUNE DISORDER OF THE BODY OF CHRIST

So far we have traced the long and rich history of our call to be God's people scattered in the world for the welfare of our neighbor, indeed, for all of creation. History and Scripture reveal the dogged persistence of this topic; it just won't go away. But history also reveals a dogged resistance on the part of the church.

If you do any additional reading on this topic, you will quickly find that many books bring up the troubled history of the concepts of vocation, calling, ministry in daily life—whatever you call it. A few paragraphs back I mentioned one of the first books that I read in this particular leg of my journey. I quoted the footnote in the first sentences of *The Equipping Pastor* by Stevens and Collins that opened my eyes to the number of years and the number of people that had been dedicated to this topic (see footnote 10, above). What I concealed from you, however, was the sentence that had been footnoted. The introduction begins with the question, "*Why has there been so little progress in the liberation of the laity?* For more than thirty years [the footnote was here] the Western church has been exposed to a growing number of books and resources focused on the release of every member of the church for ministry and mission. . . . But this proliferation of information has produced very little change in church life."[20] Since this book was

---

19. Searching "spiritual leadership" on the Internet will yield nearly a million results. The International Institute for Spiritual Leadership and the Academy of Management's "Management, Spirituality, and Religion" interest group are typical of the groups that are forming. Books published are numerous, but they include Fry and Altman, *Spiritual Leadership,* and Benefiel, *Soul at Work.*

20. Stevens and Collins, *Equipping Pastor,* xi. Emphasis in original.

published in the early 1990s, the authors' "more than thirty years" is now more than fifty years. And considering the history sketched in this chapter, even fifty is too limited. Regardless, the authors' viewpoint is valid. For too long now, the church has been talking about releasing every member for ministry and mission, but there has been very little change in actual practice.

I have recently started calling this resistance *the autoimmune disorder of the Body of Christ*. In the medical world, an autoimmune disease is an inappropriate response of the body's immune system against substances and tissues that are normally present in and helpful for the body. There is a strong parallel in the church world. As we have seen, attention to the scattering of Christ's followers into the world is vital for the well-being of the Body of Christ (the church). Many people in many places have affirmed and worked for the full implementation of this vital and life-giving expression of the church. Yet the dogged resistance of the church shows that our immune system has gone haywire, time and again resisting it, killing it off, or letting it die from attrition.

Book after book lift up this curious behavior. William Diehl, a layperson who became a leader in the ministry of the laity era (see Miller, above) writes this searing criticism in the preface to one of his books:

> As long as I can remember, my church has been proclaiming that all believers are called to be ministers. Although we have ordained clergy, my church says that there is a priesthood of all believers. My church operates on the theory that if the congregation of believers comes together for worship, study, and fellowship, then the laity will go into the world to minister to others with the love and acceptance which God has given to them. My church has been telling me that I am to be a 'little Christ' to others with whom I come in contact. That's what my church has been saying.
>
> What has my church been doing to support my ministry in the various arenas of my life?
>
> Very little.
>
> I am now a sales manager for a major steel company. In the almost thirty years of my professional career, my church has never once suggested that there be any type of accounting of my on-the-job ministry to others. My church has never once offered to improve those skills which could make me a better minister, nor has it ever asked if I needed any kind of support in what I was doing. There has never been an inquiry into the types of ethical decisions I must face, or whether I seek to communicate the faith

to my co-workers. I have never been in a congregation where there was any type of public affirmation of a ministry in my career. In short, I must conclude that my church really doesn't have the least interest in whether or how I minister in my daily work.[21]

A few years ago I had the opportunity to attend a conference titled "Spirituality at Work" at the University of Arkansas, in their Tyson Center of Faith and Spirituality in the Workplace. The conference was billed as a place where the business community, the academic community, the non-profit community, and the faith/spiritual community could come together to dialogue about the challenges and opportunities of integrating faith and spirituality in the workplace. I'm pretty sure I was the only "faith/spiritual community leader" at the conference. Corporate leaders from Walmart, ServiceMaster, and Tyson Foods talked about how their companies are founded on spiritual principles. Academics talked about research they were doing. In the middle of the conference I realized that all of the presenters and researchers were talking about what the church calls vocation; the conference was a prime example of people outside the church stepping up and taking the lead, at least in part because of the church's failure to do so.

The number of people (not to mention publications[22]) that have sought to awaken the church to our autoimmune disorder is long. In the seemingly rare cases where someone makes progress, the efforts often died out when that person or group is no longer around.

For example: After examining the church's resistance, Miller comments that "there are some notable exceptions to this general finding,"[23] but he relegates those examples to the footnotes. One of the few churches listed in the footnote is a congregation in the denomination I am part of, not far from where I live. Having heard so much criticism of the church for its failures, I was eager to see what a notable exception might look like. I looked up the congregation's webpage, but found not a single reference to ministry in daily life or any of its synonyms. Curious, I contacted the congregation only to be told, "Oh, that was a former pastor's project. He's no longer at our church, so we don't do that anymore."

Not to be defeated, I looked up the pastor and talked with him by phone. He told me that his job title had been the Equipping Pastor, and his

21. Diehl, *Real Life*, v–vi.

22. See especially chapter five of Miller, *God at Work*, "Response of the Church and the Theological Academy to FAW."

23. Miller, *God at Work*, 80.

role was to help people live their faith in their workplace. He reported his sense that most people saw faith as interacting in daily life, but on a very superficial level. He said that people weren't asking the questions he was trying to address. In addition, he said they were puzzled by his title and his role; they jokingly called him the Whipping Pastor.

My own journey has been similar to the Whipping Pastor's. Most recently, as I began reading books on the subject, more than once I thought, *I remember talking about this in seminary.* At other times I found myself regretting that I had not implemented what I had learned in seminary; I wished that I had been exposed to the ideas I've found in the books I've read recently. I sensed that the congregations I served would have been much more vital, much more intriguing places had I focused more on scattered ministries. In a very real way, this leg of my journey has opened my eyes to my own long, rich, and troubled history with the topic. At the same time, I have found that my history is not at all unique. We have been stubbornly resistant to both the premise and the promise of this essential characteristic of the church's purpose.

Perhaps this resistance has something to do with the way that we imagine our roles in the church. Let's take a look at that in the next chapter.

5

Imagining a Better Way

In chapter 3 we looked at the Bible's understanding of ministry, who does it, and when and where it takes place. We found that the two-tiered system of lay and clergy is not serving us well, especially since as God's people, claimed in the waters of baptism, we are all *klēros* (heirs, priests, ministers and saints), and we are all *laos* (the chosen people of God). Given the promise of the priesthood of all believers, and given the autoimmune disorder of the Body of Christ that undermines our attempts to equip the saints for the work of ministry, it's time to look for a more helpful way to look at our roles.

This chapter will propose a better way (or at least an alternate way) to talk about life and ministry as the gathered and scattered church. First, though, we need to look at an objection that is often raised when people start talking about empowering the scattered church. We cannot move to the better way to talk about our roles without first bringing this objection into the light. If this objection remains hidden and unchecked it will continue to undo any and all work aimed at equipping all the baptized for both gathered and scattered ministries. This objection is often raised in the form of a simple question.

ARE PASTORS IRRELEVANT OR UNBIBLICAL?

In a good many books and in the conversations I have had, especially when the topic is the perceived difference between those who are ordained and those who are not, one critical question often arises: Is this nothing more than a Trojan horse for someone's lingering doubts or suspicions about pastors? It is surprising how frequently the topic of anticlericalism crops up.

For example, in a chapter devoted to a discussion of the term *laity*, Richard Mouw acknowledges the difference between the laity and the clergy, but he struggles to avoid the inferior status that the term *laity* often carries. Late in the chapter he says, "Some readers may believe that they have detected an 'anticlerical' bias in certain of [the foregoing] comments. Before going any further, I think it important to address this issue. To adapt an old formula: some of my best friends are members of the clergy."[1] He adds, "I am convinced that the Christian church very much needs an educated clergy."[2] Mouw's section on anticlericalism is only one of many.[3]

Based on everything that has been said so far, one might wonder if I am on the verge of renouncing my ordination or proposing the eradication of the office of pastor. If Luther could get away with saying that the orders of pope, bishop, priest, and monk, are sinful orders like robbery, usury, and prostitution, why shouldn't I? One might think that is my bias, but such an assumption would be unfounded.

When the discussion of equipping all the baptized for ministry comes up, why do we jump so quickly to an assumption that what is being discussed is the dismantling of the pastoral office? Why do authors of books on ministry in daily life feel it necessary to defend themselves against charges of anticlericalism? Might this reaction be a symptom of the autoimmune disorder of the Body of Christ? Might it be that emphasis on the ministry of the whole people of God is seen as a threat to the traditional roles and responsibilities of pastors, and therefore needs to be killed?

Because this reaction happens, these questions linger and need to be addressed: Do we need to get rid of pastors and just let people do the ministry they are called to? Or would it be more helpful to find different terms to describe our various roles?

---

1. Mouw, *Holy Worldliness*, 26.

2. Ibid., 27.

3. See Stevens, *Other Six Days*, 52–53; Page *All God's People*, 92–95; or Everist, *Where in the World*, 123.

CLERICALISM MAY BE PRESENT BUT
ANTICLERICALISM IS NOT HELPFUL

An unpublished workbook related to the book, *The Laity in Ministry: The Whole People of God for the Whole World*, suggests that some pastors "are threatened by the possibility that their familiar (sometimes authoritarian) patterns will be challenged, and they may be pressured to learn new ways of thinking and acting. Some wonder whether really empowered laity will cause their pastoral role to be unnecessary."[4]

When the topic of anticlericalism comes up, it is possible that insecurity plays a role. It may be that the real sentiments at work are, "If I don't do ministry for the people, then why am I here? Why are they paying me?" The corollary to that is, of course, "If I'm not necessary then they are going to fire me." Ogden describes very similar questions:

> One of the consequences of urging pastors to shift from the role of teacher/caregiver to equipping leader is a crisis of identity. If I am not the one on whom people must rely, then who am I? Upon what is my worth and value based?[5]

Faith Goes to Work begins with a pointed description of this resistance. Barely three pages into the first essay, Edward White writes:

> Why doesn't the church take the vocation of its own members seriously? The answer, I believe, is because it is against the perceived self-interest of everyone concerned to do so! It is against the perceived self-interest of the clergy, the laity, the theological seminaries, the institutional church, and society at large.[6]

White then notes that some clergy feel the need to be in control of all that happens in a congregation. I would offer a more charitable view of this tendency by saying that pastors feel responsible for their congregations. Building on his critical assertion, though, White notes "the weekday lives of parishioners in the world are beyond the control of the clergy. Indeed, most clergy are largely unfamiliar with the worlds in which parishioners work." He also notes that since clergy are answerable to their members, "it behooves them to confine themselves to meeting the traditional expectations

---

4. Broholm, and Hoffman, "Empowering Laity." The sections are not numbered, and the page numbers begin at "1" with each new section, which makes specific page references impossible. This quote is from the third page of the essay, "Consciousness-Raising."

5. Ogden, *Unfinished Business*, 159.

6. White, "Sunday-Monday Gap," 5.

of the membership." If the traditional expectation is that pastors are supposed to be (in his words) "the professional 'need meeter,'"—even though (as we found) that is not necessarily the expectation of all members—then in order to keep their jobs, pastors will focus on that which is most likely to keep them employed. White adds, "Job security is a powerful motivator."[7] If you want to see how resistance is manifested among members, seminaries, the institutional church, and society at large, then pick up a copy of this book. The above charges that White levels against pastors are more than enough for our purposes. While I wouldn't choose to describe the resistance at work among pastors in the pointed language that White uses—in fact, among the pastors I talked to I found a pronounced desire to be better equippers—he certainly brings the issue of resistance to the surface.[8]

White shines a harsh light on dynamics that may be at work among clergy. If what he says has any validity, then perhaps *clericalism* can be defined as the embodiment of importance, power, and self-justification. If clericalism is at work in our congregations, then perhaps *anticlericalism* is an appropriate response. But anticlericalism in the sense of "let's just get rid of pastors" is not in the church's best interest. It is more helpful to consider healthy and appropriate roles in both the gathered church and the scattered church.

A METAPHOR FOR A BETTER WAY

Even though anticlericalism comes up when the work of the scattered church is explored, I don't think anybody is seeking to eliminate the office of pastor. Ultimately, the dismantling of the pastoral office would be a pipe dream at best and harmful at worst. There are simply too many years of history that we would need to undo; there are too many expectations that we would have to overcome. As we have seen, Christianity started as an underground movement with diffuse leadership. As is the case with contemporary movements, diffuse leadership makes it difficult for oppositional forces to track down and eliminate leaders and thereby kill the movement. On the other hand, when underground movements survive those who resist them, they become organizations, and organizations need leaders. The

7. Ibid., 5–6.

8. See also Ogden, *Unfinished Business*, 111–29, for a description of pastors who operate under an unhealthy dependency model.

question is: What kind of leaders do we want and need? And what do the relationships between the leaders and the followers look like?

Let me offer a metaphor that provides a powerful image for an alternative way of being a pastor. If any of what was described in the first half of this chapter is true, we could picture the pastor as a professional wakeboarder.

Sean O'Brien, one of wakeboarding's most stylish riders, is also a coach and contest judge. With Orlando as a background, Sean makes wakeboarding look amazing.

Watching pastors at work, it's really not hard to imagine pastors like this. Listen as we offer a table blessing: our prayers are eloquent, they pull together images and issues in wonderful and sometimes poetic ways, and we get our strokes when people remark, "Wonderful prayer, Pastor." I remember one such prayer in which I mentioned the rain falling outside and tied it to God's ongoing care for creation. Someone actually remarked to me afterward about what an eloquent prayer I had offered. Watching pastors at work, members may think what I think when I look at the above picture: "I could never do that." In fact, members have told me that they could never pray as eloquently as I do. Is it any wonder, then, that they continually call on us to offer prayers? Pastors can sometimes be like professional wakeboarders showing off for an admiring crowd.

I have to admit that it would be wonderful to be a professional wakeboarder. I'd like to experience the thrill of jumping a wake and spinning 360 degrees in the air. I imagine it's fun to be able to show off like that. But that's not the kind of pastor I want to be.

Shortly after the eloquent prayer I just mentioned, I realized that I had become a professional pray-er. I realized that prayers that do the equivalent of spinning 360 degrees in the air do a disservice to the people I serve. In response, I intentionally sought to lower the bar on my prayers. My goal was to generate a new response from members: I hoped they would walk away thinking, *I could do that.*

We could go on to discuss how we preach, teach, give care, and many other pastoral duties. I am not arguing that we should "dumb down" preaching and other pastoral acts. In fact (and as an example), I'm in favor of excellent, transformational preaching. It takes training and experience to do that. But I would argue against taking such pride in being professionals in our field that we inadvertently leave people in our wake, disempowered. To continue with the example of preaching, it is possible to provide excellent, engaging preaching *and* to teach people how to speak to the faith in their own terms, in their own settings.

What kind of a pastor do you want? What kind of a pastor do you want to be? I prefer to find joy working for the success of others, watching people get the hang of being a pray-er, a speaker of the faith, an interpreter of Scripture, and a minister in the activities and relationships of their everyday lives. That doesn't have the thrill of spinning in theological loops, but it is much more satisfying.

IN SEARCH OF NEW LANGUAGE

The United Methodist Church has produced a concise and balanced approach to the understanding of ministry that is very helpful for us as we look for new language for our various roles:

> Through baptism, God calls and commissions persons to the general ministry of all Christian believers (see 1992 Book of Discipline, ¶¶101–07). This ministry, in which we participate both individually and corporately, is the activity of discipleship. It is grounded upon the awareness that we have been called into a new relationship not only with God, but also with the world. *The task of Christians is to embody the gospel and the church in the world. We exercise our calling as Christians by prayer, by witnessing to the good news of salvation in Christ, by caring for and serving other*

people, and by working toward reconciliation, justice, and peace, in the world. This is the universal priesthood of all believers.

From within this general ministry of all believers, God calls and the church authorizes some persons for the task of representative ministry (see 1992 Book of Discipline, ¶¶108–110). *The vocation of those in representative ministry includes focusing, modeling, supervising, shepherding, enabling, and empowering the general ministry of the church.* Their ordination to Word, Sacrament, and Order or consecration to diaconal ministries of service, justice, and love is grounded in the same baptism that commissions the general priesthood of all believers.[9]

Rather than eliminating clergy and elevating the laity, I prefer to hold on to the tension that the Methodists have described. God calls and commissions us to the general ministry of all Christian believers. At the same time, within this general ministry God calls and the church authorizes some persons for the task of equipping and empowering the ministry of all believers.

To put that a little more concisely, and as a reminder of the long, rich, and troubled history of this topic (chapter 4), almost fifty years ago Elton Trueblood offered a helpful way to overcome this dichotomy: "The ministry is for all who are called to share in Christ's life, *the pastorate is for those who possess the peculiar gift of being able to help other men and women to practice any ministry to which they are called.*"[10]

Like other authors, I share the sentiment that it would be helpful to retire the terms *clergy* and *laity* since they tend to reinforce unhelpful stereotypes and expectations. These terms also exacerbate the autoimmune disorder of the Body of Christ and undermine our ability to equip all God's people for the call to ministry that we receive in baptism. In fact, the careful reader may have noted that I try to stay away from using *clergy* and *laity* in this book. (Where I have not been able to stay away from them is in quoting other authors or in talking about the tension as it currently exists.) Simply toning down the use of these two terms, though, won't change widely held perceptions. I propose adding language to our vocabulary. Perhaps new language will give us new ways to expand our understanding of the ministry of all God's people.

---

9. *Book of Resolutions.* 939–40. Italics added.

10. Trueblood, *Incendiary Fellowship*, 41, as quoted in Ogden, *Unfinished Business*, 133. Emphasis in original.

This new language arises directly out of chapter 1. We are *church* not only when we gather in one place, we are also *church* when we scatter into the world. We are an expression of God's kingdom (dream) when we are gathered; we are also an expression of God's dream when we are scattered as the agents and instruments of God's dream. Given that, then, instead of talking about *clergy* and *laity*, and instead of talking about ordained ministers and lay ministers, I propose the use of *gathered ministers* and *scattered ministers*. At various times, we are ministers to and among the people of God when we are the Body of Christ gathered. At other times and among other people we are ministers (*diakonos*, servants) when we are the Body of Christ scattered. What needs to be avoided here is thinking that gathered ministers = clergy and scattered ministers = lay. The whole purpose of this language is to overcome the dichotomy that holds us back.

Here's an easy exercise to explore the meaning of this new language: name some gathered ministers. *Pastor* is likely the first role that comes to mind. It doesn't take much effort, though, to move beyond that. Communion assistants, lectors, Sunday school teachers, youth workers, nursery workers, and similar roles will naturally come to mind. All of that is good. There are a variety of gathered ministers in the life of the church, and they are necessary and helpful roles; for people who fulfill such roles we give thanks.

Now try this exercise, which based on earlier comments you should be able to do: name some scattered ministers. Parents might be an easy answer, as well as nurses, doctors, and teachers. We can use the quote from Luther in chapter 4 to add, "husbands and wives, boys and girls, lords and ladies, governors, regents, judges, officeholders, farmers, citizens, etc." The number and variety of scattered ministers is astonishing and encouraging. As the church scattered, we serve as God's ministers, that is, we offer care, comfort, service, support, encouragement, and other Christ-like acts in an amazing number of ways and circumstances.

Note what happens when we drop *clergy* and *laity* and talk instead about gathered ministers and scattered ministers. As the Methodist *Book of Resolutions* says, some of the gathered ministers are ordained (that is, consecrated or set aside) for the particular purpose of "focusing, modeling, supervising, shepherding, enabling, and empowering the general ministry of the [gathered and scattered] church." But not all of the gathered ministers are ordained. Everyday, ordinary people serve as gathered ministers as well.

Notice as well what happens when we talk about scattered ministers. Obviously everyday, ordinary people come to mind when we list the roles of scattered ministers. What we might not see right off the bat, though, is that scattered ministers are not lay persons at all—at least not in the sense of being uneducated, amateur, or unqualified. In our scattered ministry roles, it is likely that we are the highly trained experts. In fact, if a pastor were to dabble in the scattered ministry roles of a stockbroker or teacher, the pastor would immediately be identified as "a lay person."

That said, there is one more facet to scattered ministers that we dare not overlook: ordained ministers serve as scattered ministers as well. They might not be qualified to design a structurally sound building or even to swing a hammer to build one, but pastors are scattered ministers too. They are husbands and wives, parents, adult children of aging parents, citizens, consumers, and neighbors.

TAKING THE NEXT STEP

If the concept of gathered and scattered church is helpful, and if we extend that to talk about gathered and scattered ministers, then there is one additional step that we can take to broaden our description of *church*. As gathered and scattered church, in the roles of gathered and scattered ministers, we also engage in gathered and scattered *ministries*.

We can go through the same exercises we used earlier. Name some gathered ministries. That's easy, as worship and faith formation will roll right off our tongues. Serving on boards and committees are familiar gathered ministries. Stewardship, evangelism, even administrative support and property management are unglamorous gathered ministries, but they are important. (We'll explore some of those in chapter 8 as they will likely take on other forms when viewed from the perspective of a scattered church.) It gets trickier when we look at supporting a food pantry or a clothes closet. While these ministries often serve people outside the congregation, they would likely qualify as gathered ministries, at least in the sense that they are ministries that we undertake together, as opposed to ministries that we offer in our everyday lives. Recruiting members to serve supper at the shelter or to participate in a mission trip can be seen as gathered ministries in that sense as well.

Now name some scattered ministries. This too should be easier now. All we have to do is look back at the previous section, find the list of scattered ministers, and translate those roles in terms of scattered ministries. All that parents, voters, office workers, law enforcement officers, legislators, farmers, friends, sanitation workers, and baggage handlers do could begin what would become a very long list.

As we just saw, the differences between lay and clergy disappear when we talk in terms of gathered ministries and scattered ministries. Pastors perform gathered ministries, to be sure, and there are valid and necessary reasons for that. But pastors engage in scattered ministries as well. Even if, like me, they "live the church 24/7," they are still spouses, parents, friends, voters, and consumers. Given this, the church has a neglected but critical calling to equip and empower pastors as scattered ministers. This is often lost when the commonly held assumption is that "we pay the pastor to do ministry," especially when that ministry is limited to what pastors do in and for the gathered church.

Similarly, lay people perform gathered ministries as well, and in so doing, they engage in valid and necessary ministries. But it is highly likely that 99.9 percent of their time is committed to scattered ministries. Considering this, we have an overwhelming case for creating an equipping community, so that we—all of us—equip one another for the work of ministry, until all of us come to the measure of the full stature of Christ (Eph 4:13). Which just happens to be the topic for the next chapter.

6

Living out the Biblical Imagination

From the very beginning I have held out the promise that pursuing the vision of the ministry of all the baptized doesn't depend on creating new initiatives, asking people to do something more, or raising more money. In fact, as I stated, pursuing this vision may call us to let go of some of the pressing parish concerns that keep our attention riveted on the gathered church and gathered ministries.

Equally counterintuitive to some may be the realization that a focus on the scattered church is not something that needs to be added or restored to the life of a congregation. As we found in chapter 2, it is already present. Many of our members have a strong sense that they are called to ministry in their relationships and activities. The call to ministry in the world is abundantly present in prayers, in liturgical responses, in hymns, in Scripture, and sermons. We talk the talk, big time, but as we found, we don't always walk the walk. For understandable reasons and for sinful reasons (and for reasons that might be both at the same time), we turn inward and focus on ourselves; we focus on what we want and what we think we need in order to thrive—or maybe just to survive.

This chapter looks at the biblical call to deny ourselves (which, in this case, will be applied to our corporate sense of self), and how that can free us to love and serve our neighbors. Acknowledging the reality that the gathered church is important, needs to be healthy, and is worthy of our attention, we look at the future from a both/and rather than an either/or perspective. We cling to the resurrection promise that dying to ourselves will bring new life.

DYING TO THE URGE TO SURVIVE

When I think about the tendency to turn inward, one of the most appropriate Scripture passages is found in each of the four gospels. I like the version in Mark:

> If any want to become my followers, let them deny themselves and take up their cross and follow me. For those who want to save their life will lose it, and those who lose their life for my sake, and for the sake of the gospel, will save it. For what will it profit them to gain the whole world and forfeit their life? Indeed, what can they give in return for their life? Those who are ashamed of me and of my words in this adulterous and sinful generation, of them the Son of Man will also be ashamed when he comes in the glory of his Father with the holy angels. (Mark 8:34–38)

I am willing to bet that you skimmed over that passage since it is so familiar. We know that we are called to lose our lives for Christ's sake. However, when we apply this passage to what we have learned so far, something surprising and maybe even unsettling happens.

If we start with the premise that pastors and members alike are aware that ministry is happening in our daily lives, then it's a short leap for us to move from "dying to ourselves" to "serving others for the life of the world." Those who preach and those who listen know that we are called to die to ourselves for the sake of the other. Where I intend to push the envelope, maybe even step on toes, is in regard to the call to die to the corporate life of the gathered church—at least as we have known it—for the sake of the world.

IS BUSYNESS OUR ENEMY?

In an article in the secular press entitled "Are Sundays Dying?" the author notes that as we edge "ever closer to a machine-tethered, work-chained, gruel-fed world governed by corporate automatons," Sunday is "beginning to look more and more like just another day of the work week."[1] Smart

---

1. Jacobs, "Are Sundays Dying?" third paragraph and last paragraph. It's interesting

phones, email, and text messages not only connect us to one another, they keep us tethered to work. Manufacturers are often in the office on Sunday because for their factories, located in Asia, it's already Monday morning and if the orders aren't in, the company loses a day of productivity. It's a wonder stock brokers can ever sleep because in this globally connected world, a market is always open somewhere.

When I talk to rural pastors they tell me about the incredible distance that people travel each day to take kids to school or extra-curricular activities, to get to and from work, to shop, or to participate in community activities. "People just don't have the time to do something else for the church." Others complain about the lack of priority that members give to participation in the life of the church, often describing athletic activities in particular as competition for the church. All the while we keep asking people to do more and more in and through the congregation's programs because keeping the gears turning and the (financial) wheels greased is what seems most important, even though we are painfully aware that "everybody is already so busy."

Question: If we're serious about connecting faith and life in the world, if we're serious about empowering and supporting scattered ministries, why are we "competing" to take people out of the world? Dare we, instead, die to our corporate selves? Do we dare die to our preoccupation with getting people to participate in gathered ministries (especially when those are seen as something that keeps congregations vital and necessary) so that we can live out our scattered ministries in the tasks and relationships of our everyday lives? When we are the Body of Christ gathered, shouldn't we be applying the ancient practices of the church to the various vocations given to us as the Body of Christ scattered, as parents, workers, students, teammates, voters, or volunteers?

Here's what I'd like you to chew on: It is possible that congregational health and vitality will not be found in the latest program or technique that will fix what we perceive to be problems in our congregations. It is possible that finding a new style of worship that will attract more people to our pews is not the best way to reassure ourselves that our congregations are vital and necessary. It is possible that a healthy church (and I use that word in

that this article and its lament is not from the religious press, but from The Pacific Standard, a bimonthly print magazine and website, part of the non-profit Miller-McCune Center for Research, Media and Public Policy. They focus on "the nation's biggest issues—with a focus on economics, society and justice, education, and the environment—by paying particular interest to what shapes human behavior."

its broadest sense, as the people not the organization) is not defined by the numbers of participants or the amount of money in the bank. It is possible that congregational health and vitality could, instead, be defined by how well we give ourselves away as scattered ministers, in our various scattered ministries.

THE COUNTERINTUITIVE ELEPHANT IN THE ROOM

Before we move further into this chapter we need to revisit a systemic block that threatens any and all work to create an equipping environment in the gathered church. We first covered this ground in chapter 2, in the discussion of how the vitality of the institution trumps all, but it bears repeating: our systems are built to support and enhance the viability of the congregation. With this in mind, we need to talk about the elephant in the room: *working to create an equipping congregation is a counterintuitive move.* To be more precise, it is and will be counterintuitive as long as the health and the welfare of the gathered church is our primary concern. Focusing on the ministries that we do as the scattered church will not directly support the perceived vitality of the organization; in fact, such efforts will likely be seen as weakening the congregation.

For example, some pastors I talked to suggested affirming and supporting Little League parents and coaches in their ministries of promoting health and teaching cooperation and social skills. If we do that, some people will see such a move as weakening support for congregational activities. If we redefine an active member based not only on participation in and support of gathered church ministries but in how we love our neighbor, people may feel less obligated to attend our activities and fear for the congregation's longevity will take over.

It should be obvious that the starting point here is our understanding of the purpose of the church. If our purpose is solely to perpetuate our gathered ministries, then scattered ministries are and will be a threat. If, however, our purpose as the gathered church is seen through the lens of equipping the saints to be the scattered church—for the work of perpetuating God's dream—then and only then will we be able to truly celebrate and support all that we do in the ordinary roles and relationships of our lives.

IT'S A BOTH/AND QUESTION

Let's return to this chapter's opening question: Are we willing to risk losing our (corporate) life for the sake of the world? We are already giving ourselves away individually. We don't need to convince anybody to do something more to prove that, either in the church or in their daily lives. Both our congregational lives and our daily lives are rich with opportunities to serve, provide hospitality, support, love, and speak words of hope. The central question here is this: can we find the courage to hold the importance of both the gathered church and the scattered church as equal parts of a single reality?

Here's an idea: let's put the words of Isaiah 2:5 over the door that leads into our worship spaces: "Come, let us walk in the light of the Lord." That passage speaks to all that happens when we are drawn into the Spirit's heart. As we walk in the light of the Lord, broken lives are healed by words of forgiveness, hungry people are fed by the Lord's Supper, isolated individuals are united with the people of God in all time and in all places, and people lost in the vagaries of life receive hope and strength in prayer and in the mutual consolation of the saints. But now imagine that on the inside of the worship space, over those same doors, people would see these words as they leave the worship space: "Come, let us walk in the light of the Lord."

Both dynamics are at work in the church. Gathered by the Spirit, faith moves life's center from earth to heaven. At the same time, scattered by the Spirit, love moves life's center from heaven to earth. Both movements, both dynamics, are critical. Let me say this once again: What we do as the gathered church is important. We have a good handle on proclaiming the gospel and celebrating the sacraments. We plug away at offering Bible studies, small group opportunities, and other faith formation activities. We have long lists of things (aka, Time and Talent sheets) that people can and will do in and through the church. We regularly affirm those who participate and serve in the church. From all appearances, we're doing pretty well with the gathering dynamic, but we're not so sure how to support the scattering. If we were, the woman at Walgreens would have answered my friend's question quickly and confidently, "Of course my congregation values and supports my ministry here."

SHAPING A PEOPLE-CENTERED, WORLD-CENTERED CHURCH

In chapter 4 of his book, Greg Ogden identifies four shifts that he says will enable the church to restore the understanding that ministry belongs to the whole people of God. At the beginning of chapter 5 he says that these four shifts "can be summarized in one sentence: *We need to move from a pastor-centered to a people-centered ministry.*"[2] Yes! If we are sincere about wanting to equip the saints for their ministries both as the gathered church and as the scattered church, then Ogden hits the proverbial nail on the head.

But is it possible that Ogden did not take this movement far enough? I propose taking Ogden's one-sentence summary and expanding it. We need to move from thinking of the church as being pastor-centered to being people-centered, *and* we need to move from being church-centered to being world-centered.

I developed the chart on p. 98 based on discoveries that have come to light in my recent journey through this topic. This chart describes what we already know well, and it describes a perspective that we don't know as well, if at all. It's something of a two-dimensional spectrum. In the left column, from top to bottom, are some pastor-centered and church-centered perspectives from which we most often operate. The right column describes another spectrum from being people-centered at the top to being world-centered at the bottom. The right column, then, provides counterpoints to what is on the left, and in doing that provides the second dimension of the spectrum. Reading this chart from top to bottom and from side to side provides a number of contrasting comparisons, it provides a number of new ways of looking at long-held assumptions and practices, and it opens some new possibilities for the life of the church.

---

2. Ogden, *Unfinished Business*, 111. Emphasis in original.

Pastor-centered	People-centered
• Pastor knows all, shapes all	• Pastor is a player-coach
• Pastor preaches (seminary trained)	• People witness to life in the world
• Pastor is paid to do ministry	• People are empowered for ministry
• Pastor "lives the church"	• Pastor is bifocal, maybe bi-vocational
• Pastor is the most active member	• Definition of *active member* changes
• People are consumers	• People are doers
• Ministry happens mostly in the church	• Ministry happens mostly in the world
• Ministry is easier to report on but limited	• Ministry is unlimited but harder to report on
• People are commissioned for church work	• People are commissioned for daily life
• Asking people to do more at church	• Affirming what people do in daily life
• Keeping doors open is most important	• Sending people out is most important
• Inviting others to church	• Meeting/loving others in the world
Church-centered	**World-centered**

We know the items in the upper left corner well. This was the reality that many pastors described in chapter 2. In this corner the people look to the pastor for just about everything. Pastors interpret the Bible and preach because they are seminary trained. Pastors are the professional believers and so they are asked to say the blessing at meetings and meals. In my first call, I was expected to be at every committee meeting. That wasn't the bad part; the problem was that the committees wouldn't make a decision until they heard my opinion, and they usually followed my lead. Who is expected to make the hospital visits? The pastor. Sometimes the examples of a pastor-centered ministry run to the ridiculous. For example, in my first call, one Sunday morning as I was preparing for worship, someone came in the front door, tracked me down and reported, "Pastor, there's a dead bird on the sidewalk."

Ogden recommends moving from the upper left to the upper right corner of the chart. Part of what he missed, though, is another equally problematic dynamic at work, and that is the church-centered ministry. When a pastor-centered ministry is considered insufficient or passé, the likely move is to focus on what we do as the gathered church. The lower left corner of the chart describes a contrast to the pastor-centered ministry, but many times these factors don't go beyond reworking current assumptions in order to empower members to do things that pastors are expected to do in the upper left corner of the chart. We feel better about this model of church because the people are involved, but the focus is still on the activities of the gathered church. The lower left corner of the chart, by itself, is not an adequate embodiment of God's dream.

As Ogden suggests, the upper right corner of the chart provides some helpful contrasts to both the upper left and the lower left corners. In a people-centered ministry, the pastor doesn't just do things on behalf of or for the members. The role of a player-coach is instructive.[3] A coach stands on the sidelines and sends signals onto the field to tell the players what to do. Player-coaches provide guidance to other teammates, but they are also on the field playing a position. In a people-centered ministry, the pastor isn't the only one who applies faith to life; the people also get involved, testifying to the role of faith in the world. Professional staff members are not the only ones who do ministry; the people are empowered as well. The pastor is no longer the most active member. In fact, the definition of *active member* changes to include the ministry that all God's people perform in the world.

The final piece that Ogden's proposal missed is the lower right corner, a world-centered ministry. This corner provides strong contrasts to our usual understanding of *church*. This corner embraces the "giving our life" imperative from Mark 8. A world-centered model affirms that ministry doesn't just happen as the gathered church. In fact, in terms of sheer volume, ministry happens mostly in the world, in the activities and relationships of our everyday lives. While a church-centered model makes it easy to count and report on what we're doing, ministry in that model is limited to the few hours a week that people can squeeze into their schedules. A world-centered ministry extends beyond our wildest imaginations to include serving meals as staff in a restaurant or as parents in a family, repairing automobiles or furnaces, teaching children in a school or in our homes, and selling insurance so that people's lives and livelihood are protected, to name just a few. Of course when ministry expands like this, it's much harder to report on. In a world-centered ministry we don't just commission people for churchy tasks; we commission them for daily life. In a world-centered model we don't judge our vitality by how many people we bring in, but by how well prepared we send them out. While we should invite people to church when the timing and circumstances are right, we find meaning and purpose in encountering, loving, and serving people in the world.

In all likelihood, by now you're probably wondering where the sweet spot lies. Is it the bottom right corner, or at least somewhere in the right

---

3. I am indebted to Ogden and Trueblood for this image. See Ogden, *Unfinished Business*, 97–98.

column? Is it dead center? The answer may surprise you. It's not in the right column of the chart. The sweet spot may not even be in the middle. The place where we should dwell is not in any one corner, as if there is only one right way to be the church. In fact, there is no sweet spot at all, not if we look at the nature and purpose of the church with a both/and perspective.

While the left column calls our attention to ways in which we have short-circuited our calling as church, it also glosses over helpful dynamics of the gathered church. There is nothing wrong with pastors using their seminary training to preach informed and transforming sermons. There is nothing wrong with commissioning people as Sunday school teachers or mission trip participants. And there is nothing better about a bi-vocational pastor or performing scattered ministries. Each of the items on the chart has purpose and value. It's just that when we get stuck in one of the corners—even if by some miracle we found ourselves stuck in the lower right corner—problems emerge.

For now it's enough to admit that most of us have been stuck somewhere in the left column, often in an effort to "save our own life." For now it's enough to admit that it would be helpful to move to the right column. When we attempt to change long-held, deeply embedded perspectives (the left column), sometimes it is necessary to swing the pendulum hard to the other side in order to shake ourselves loose from prior ways of doing things, and then later settle into a more balanced position. I did that in my last congregation by employing the tagline, "Out of Zion, God Shines Forth." Notice that the tagline doesn't affirm the both/and reality that God also shines *in* Zion. In order to shake thinking loose, we chose to swing hard to the external reality. It might be that, for the short-term, leaders of congregations will need to deemphasize approaches in the left column that we know so well while we explore life in the right column.

HOW DO WE SWING THE PENDULUM?

So how do we start working on making our congregations more people-centered and world-centered? How can we create a congregational environment that supports and encourages the ministries that we all have in the work we do, in the education we pursue, in the relationships that define our lives, and in the tasks of everyday life? We'll consider this in more detail in chapter 8, but for now a few possibilities are worth considering.

Leaders who desire to create an equipping environment first need to keep people in conversation by asking relevant and probing questions. Only through such inquisitive conversations can we uncover a fuller understanding of what it means to be *church*. As a beginning point for these conversations, I propose questions related to four topics that have roots in the above chart.

Evaluating the impact of ministry

The chart makes reference to reporting. Those things that we currently report are easy to see, count, and evaluate. In the scattered church, our understanding of ministry expands considerably, but it is harder to report. So how can we find ways to evaluate and report the impact we are having in our homes, in our workplaces or schools, in our communities, and in the world? How can this be as important as reporting measurable things like attendance, income and expenses, and assets?

Some people I've talked to suggested that such reporting needs to happen weekly and in one-on-one (or at least in a small group) settings. If we are intentional about reporting weekly on the issues we are facing in our lives, about how it's gone since we were last together, or about where we've seen God at work or calling us to serve, maybe then, at the end of the year, we would be better equipped to report on ministry that goes beyond attendance and finances.

Equipping members

The chart compares the understanding that pastors are paid to do ministry to the Ephesians 4 vision of equipping and empowering all the baptized for ministry. How can congregations best equip members for ministry? While pastors should be thoroughly prepared for parish ministry, how can we make an equal commitment to equipping all God's people for ministry in their daily lives? Seminaries are making efforts to expand their educational offerings to include all the baptized through online education. How can seminaries and judicatories equip congregational leaders so that they can equip the people for their scattered ministries? (We will look at answers to some of these questions in chapters 7 and 8.)

One piece of the equipping puzzle is to change the mindset of the congregation. We are accustomed to seeing membership in terms of participation in gathered church activities. How can we redefine what it means to be an active member? What would it mean to stop seeing *church* in terms of competing for the time and energy of our people? How can we change our assumptions so that we see our members as being active Christians in the tasks they do daily and in the relationships that define their lives? Changing our mindset will go a long way toward our ability to equip the saints for their ministries.

Affirming our scattered ministries

In several places the left column of the chart refers to the fact that we are good at affirming and supporting our gathered ministries. How can we affirm our scattered ministries at least as much as we affirm our gathered ministries? How can the ministry that people are doing every day be lifted up in the same way that the ministry of pastors and other staff in the church is often emphasized?

At a gathering of a regional judicatory, the person in charge asked that all pastors who serve a congregation stand up. We applauded them for their service. Then the leader asked that all pastors serving in specialized ministries (hospitals, colleges and the like) stand, and we applauded them for their service. Then all retired pastors were asked to stand and we thanked them for their service. In the next breath, the leader went on to the next item of business. Meanwhile, two-thirds of the people in the room were not ordained, and so we completely glossed over the countless ways that they serve God's purposes in the world. What would it take to recognize and celebrate the ministry of all the baptized?

We expect pastors and church staff to put in 40–60 hours of ministry a week (or more) but how many thousands of hours could we celebrate if we include the ministry we all do in our daily lives? How might pastors learn to live out the metaphor of teaching people to wakeboard from chapter 5 rather than performing for them or on their behalf? How might we learn to tell stories of the ministries our members are performing every day?

Equipping congregations

Several of the items in the above chart have implications for the structure of our congregations, our priorities, and what staff members do. In order to move toward the right column, what structural and programmatic changes would help us become equipping congregations—congregations that focus on empowering and sending people into the world to minister in God's name? What would that mean for preaching and teaching? What effect might it have on how we develop job descriptions, congregational structures, and priorities? What would have to change in order to evaluate the important things we do as the gathered church based on the impact those activities and priorities have as the scattered church?

Try this at home: go back to the chart above and, using the up and down, left and right comparisons, add some questions of your own to those I proposed here. There are many more categories and questions embedded in those comparisons. Questions about systems and cultures (see "Paying attention to the system—and the culture" in chapter 7) that trap us in any one of the corners of the above chart would be especially helpful to discuss with people in your congregation. Let me be clear: I am not suggesting that you need to do something more than you are already doing; in fact, as I have said before it might be a matter of doing less. What I am suggesting is that questions such as these can help us view what we are currently doing with new eyes, and they can help us to see new ways to live out God's dream in the world.

THIS IS BASED ON PROMISE AND HOPE

One of the most encouraging words that came out of my conversations was to hear others affirm that God is already at work in the world. God is working to restore the world to what it was intended to be, and God is doing that work through us. God is working through the things that we do as the gathered church and we should celebrate that. What we tend to overlook, though, is that God is working in more ways than we can imagine, much less count, in the things we do as the scattered church. How can we train ourselves to look for that activity, to name it, to support and empower people for the part they play, and then to send them out to do it? It will take some "dying to ourselves" in order to pull this off. But then, it seems to me, the passage from Mark 8 can be applied to the congregation's life as much as it can be applied to individuals.

From where I sit, doing only what we are doing now will serve to keep our focus on "saving our lives" as congregations. We know what keeping our life looks like. It looks pretty much like everything in the left column of the above chart. We also know where "saving our life" has gotten us.

On the other hand, losing our life for the sake of the world is scary and, if we're honest, a foreign prospect. Which expectations, traditions, and activities are blocking our ability to imagine new ways to free people for ministry in the world? Are we willing to let go of pet projects that only bolster our congregation's ego? Are we willing to learn new ways to count, define, report, and value ministries that happen in our lives every day?

Once again, here is the promise: congregations that are willing to lose their lives for the sake of the gospel—for the sake of the good news about God's love for the world—will find new life and vitality. They will find new purpose and meaning.

Interlude: Connecting the Blessing and the Purpose

By Forrest Walden
founder and CEO of Iron Tribe Fitness

I found myself standing in the middle of a dump in Honduras, watching the people who call it "home." A pregnant woman walked in front of me, dragging a trash bag while battling birds and cows for her next meal. My mind flashed to my wife, Mendy, who was at home and pregnant as well. Their circumstances could not have been farther apart.

I thought about everything I had acquired up to that point—the vacation home at the beach, the BMW, the businesses that were opening and running successfully—and I had one of those "God moments." I felt God clearly asking, *Forrest, what are you going to do with your time, talents, and treasure? It has to be something bigger than you.*

Up to that point my life had been an insatiable pursuit of success. It consumed every fiber of my being as I sought to live a life of significance. Although I had been raised in a Christian home and had accepted Christ as my Lord and Savior very early in life I was still pursuing significance through achievement. The Christianity of my childhood seemed to be on the periphery of my life.

Growing up, my main goal was to play college football. When that didn't materialize I turned to bodybuilding, which led me into a career in personal training. Before I knew what happened I was a master franchisee of a national fitness brand overseeing fifty-five locations in three states. I was experiencing more success than I had ever dreamt about.

I consistently write in a journal and when I review what I wrote while I was building my business, one common theme emerges: the question *Why?* "God, why have you chosen to bless me?" was a common entry as I was struggling to understand why I was experiencing so much favor.

Somewhere along the way I began to subconsciously answer the *Why?* question myself. I came up with answers like, "I'm successful because I deserve it, because I'm working harder than anyone else, because I'm pushing myself with books and audio programs." Now I see that God was using those questions to prepare me to hear an entirely different answer.

THE WAKE UP CALL

On February 7, 2006, I heard a sermon from our soon-to-be-announced pastor, David Platt, which absolutely riveted me and hit me squarely between the eyes. It was one of those experiences where I may as well have been the only person in the room. That morning God clearly answered my five-year question of *Why?*

The sermon was titled, "The Ultimate Disconnect–Have we disconnected the blessings of God from the purposes of God?" The main Scripture was Psalm 67:1–2:

> May God be gracious to us and bless us
> and make his face to shine upon us,
> that your way may be known upon earth,
> your saving power among all nations.

It was a verse I was very familiar with, yet I had never fully realized the importance of the word *that* in verse 2, which unlocks the meaning of the verse. God desires to bless us so that God's way, God's salvation, may be known among all nations. The question is not, "How can I gain success?" but, "How can I most effectively make the glory of Christ known to all the nations with the life God has entrusted to me?"

I started to ponder whether all of the success I had experienced had a bigger purpose—a purpose I had missed. It was about this time that David challenged the entire congregation to spend two percent of their year, which equates to one week, on an international mission trip. That is how I ended up in a garbage dump in Honduras. That is when my life changed.

The question of *Why?* continued. I realized I had lived in a bubble my entire life and truly hadn't understood how most of the world lives. The next year I took trips to India and Sudan and my world opened up even further. I visited kids in a hospital who were dying from diarrhea and other water-born diseases so easily cured in America. Up to that point, clean water was something I had taken for granted. I never considered the millions of people who have no access to it, and how that impacts every part of their lives.

I was traveling with two really good friends from my small group at church and we were gripped by the desperate situations we were seeing. All three of us felt like God was clearly calling us to do something more than just live comfortable lives. Back home we met weekly for prayer in my office, and as we prayed we continued to feel drawn to do something about what we had seen. My pastor continued to teach that we have a command to care for others and that this command isn't just for a few in the church who are called. We are all called. So the three of us decided to do something about what we had seen, with the help of the Holy Spirit.

Neverthirst (www.neverthirstwater.org) was born and our goal was to bring clean and living water to the poorest and least evangelized places on earth. Since the start of the ministry in 2008, we've been blessed to be able to raise more than eight million dollars and develop over 3,000 water projects, which serve roughly 300,000 people in Asia and Africa. Neverthirst digs deep-water wells, provides filtration systems, and offers hygiene education in South Sudan, Central African Republic, India, Nepal and Cambodia. Everything is coordinated through local churches, which allows many other Christians to share the good news—providing not only *physical water* but also the *living water* found in Jesus Christ.

Once we started Neverthirst, I thought I was being called to devote all my time to the ministry, travel the world, and work on behalf of the poor. My desire for business was waning and I started to dream about selling my business so that I could work full time for Neverthirst. I could not imagine that God would have anything else in store for me except to serve this rapidly growing ministry.

A NEW WAY OF LOOKING AT MY LIFE AND WORK

At about the same time I had invited a few of my friends to work out with me in a simple gym that I built in my garage. Up to this point, my career had focused on personal training so working out as a group was new to me. We were having a blast as we got into shape together. Unexpectedly, a new business idea started to form in the back of my mind—an idea that excited and terrified me. I was afraid that I was simply responding to my old desire to be successful in a for-profit business, and that I was turning my back on everything that I had learned and that God had shown me the last few years. For over a year I oscillated back and forth over God's will for my life. I was confident that God was calling me to sell my existing business, but what I was supposed to do next wasn't clear.

Through prayer, fasting, and journaling I came to the conclusion that God had given me talents in business for a reason. Not only would it not be a sin to build a new business, I realized it was exactly what God had equipped me and called me to do! The excitement I felt about my garage gym and starting a new business was the very gifting, passion, and desire God would use to benefit others. It became clearer and clearer that working for a nonprofit ministry or building another for-profit business was not an either/or choice. I realized that God did indeed desire for me to start over in business *and* to connect the fitness business to God's larger purposes.

I sold my prior business and started over. I converted that little garage gym experiment into a brand new business concept called Iron Tribe Fitness. Instead of focusing on personal training, we live out our brand's purpose of creating fitness communities that change lives. In less than five years we built five corporately owned and operated gyms, and franchised the business in fourteen states from Miami to Seattle. My team and I have had awesome opportunities to take what I learned from that sermon on Psalm 67:1–2 and connect the blessing (business, relationships, resources) with the purpose (God's kingdom).

Throughout this process of building a business that I see as a ministry, I've learned that we as believers should pray for blessings, manage our money as good stewards, and grow our business, but then we should also hold these things with open hands and use them to bless others the way God has blessed us. I've also learned that everything I do in my life can be connected to ministry. I've talked with many of my friends who are in full-time ministry who actually think that people in the business world have more opportunities to share faith, engage in ministry, and further God's kingdom than they do!

I am now confident that my work is about more than just me. It's about more than a workout, more than a gym. Yes, our core business is to teach healthy lifestyles, and the health improvements that our clients experience have been amazing. But in an increasingly isolated and individualized culture, our business is also about encouraging fellowship and community within what we call "the tribe." Remarkably, that community helps our clients realize their health goals faster than they would on their own. Because of that sense of community, we also have seen small group Bible studies form among staff and clients. Many times clients who have not been exposed to the church have heard the gospel through these groups. My pastor actually led one of these groups at the gym where he works out and he told me that it has been a blessing to him because it is one of the few places that gets him outside of his "Christian bubble."

Finally, our business is not just about making money; it's about connecting our blessings with global needs (Psalm 67:1–2). It has been amazing to see how our clients have embraced causes that are important to us, and to see how thankful they are to be offered ways to give and be involved in issues that truly matter. We have built fundraisers into the group workouts across all our franchises. We support *Workout for Warriors* to reintegrate veterans into civilian life, using fitness as a tool. We created *Workout for Water*, which to date has raised over one million dollars for Neverthirst projects. I have also had the opportunity to lead trips to India and Cambodia with both franchisees and clients to show them the results of their fund raising. It is so amazing to allow them to experience the change they are creating in the world and then watch them as they become a mouthpiece to the rest of the tribe.

I am the founder and CEO of a national fitness franchise but I have no doubt that what I do every day to build my brand is instrumental to the missional call on my life. God is at work in every aspect of my life so that God's way may be known upon earth, and God's saving power may be known among all nations.

For more information on the development of Forrest's business, visit www.irontribefitness.com or read his book, *Iron Tribe: From Garage Hobby To Fitness Franchise*, published by Advantage Media Group, 2013.

7

Imagining an Equipping
Community

In my research for this book I came across David Miller's description of
the Faith at Work era (see chapter 4). As he describes that era, Miller
claims that people want to integrate faith and work, and to do that they
are forming groups at work for prayer and Bible study.[1] His bold statement
puzzled me as I had never seen evidence of this trend. In order to test
Miller's claim, I posted a comment on Facebook, asking my friends if they
had seen or participated in any faith at work groups.

My nephew, Forrest, replied to my post, saying that his business had
started Bible studies that included staff and clients, that they have a church
startup meeting in one of their gyms, and that his business sponsors fund-
raising events for clean water projects overseas. Forrest concluded his reply,
"My work is my ministry."

I was fascinated and encouraged by Forrest's reply, and I was eager to
hear how he had come to such a clear understanding that his work is his
ministry. I took him to lunch and he told me the story you just read.[2] His
story reveals that his pastor played a pivotal role in his journey. His story
shows that spiritual practices played a large part in his discernment. Forrest
also points out the critical role of a faith community. In Forrest's case, the
faith community can be most clearly seen in a circle of Christian friends

---

1. Miller, *God at Work*, 71–75.

2. See Prentiss and Lowe, *Radical Sending*, 81–94, for a good many first-person
stories of people who have connected faith with life.

who walked with him through his discernment, and who helped shape his call to ministry in the workplace.

This chapter deepens the conversation about how congregational leaders might imagine and shape a community that equips God's people for their scattered ministries. Of the three critical factors that show up in Forrest's story (the role of the pastor, the faith community, and spiritual practices), this chapter looks at the first two; we'll return to the third in the next chapter.

IT TAKES A VILLAGE

In the 1990s Hillary Rodham Clinton made an African proverb famous in the title of her book, *It Takes a Village*. The title is reflective of African cultures that see the task of rearing children as a community task, rather than (as we see it) the prerogative of one set of parents.

The same sentiment is true for the task of equipping the saints. In describing how to equip the saints, Paul lists pastors (or more accurately "pastor-teachers") alongside apostles, prophets, and evangelists. At the very least, then, this work belongs to a team. In a section entitled, "Equipping is Team Oriented," Sue Mallory describes a principle that undergirds her book: "The word *equipping* immediately assumes a team model—those who do the equipping and those who are being equipped. One group needs the other. They form a team."[3]

In our day, though, the teammates that Paul lists—apostles, prophets, and evangelists—are remnants of a bygone era. If we were to paraphrase Paul's language and pair it with Mallory's principle, we could say, "The gifts God gave were that some would be pastors, some directors of faith formation, some teachers, and some committee members, to equip the saints for the work of ministry, for building up the body of Christ." But even this misses the point of the rest of Paul's message: ". . . until *all of us* come to the unity of the faith and of the knowledge of the Son of God, to maturity, to the measure of the full stature of Christ . . . speaking the truth in love, we must grow up in every way into him who is the head, into Christ, from whom the whole body, joined and knit together by every ligament with which it is equipped, as each part is working properly, promotes the body's growth in building itself up in love" (Eph 4:13, 15–16, italics added).

---

3. Mallory, *Equipping Church*, 22.

Davida Foy Crabtree, a United Church of Christ pastor, puts it this way:

> It has come to be popular to describe the role of ordained minis-
> ters in the renewed church as "equippers of the saints." I have come
> to question this model insofar as it implies that equipping is a one-
> way street. In fact, the laity [at my church] have done as much to
> equip me as I have to equip them. They have taught me about their
> lives and about the shape of work . . . They have taught me skills in
> education, group process, organizational development, and lead-
> ership training. Sometimes this has been intentional teaching on
> their part. Often it has been their willingness to express a need,
> and their desire for me to respond to that need. We have equipped
> one another for ministry.[4]

It's not the pastor's job to know all, see all, and do all when it comes to equipping the saints for ministry; rather, it takes a village.[5] It is the work of the people to equip one another for ministry. As Paul says in 1 Corinthians 12, we need each other, and each part of the body has a particular role to play. That is as true for equipping the saints as it is for any other endeavor of the church.

THE ROLE OF LEADERS—INCLUDING PASTORS

That said, though, we need to return to the role of leaders in the congrega-
tion, and in particular, the role of the pastor. While equipping the saints for the work of ministry belongs to the whole Body, that does not mean the pastor has no part. To the contrary, the pastor has a vital role. And other leaders in our congregations, be they staff members or volunteers, have roles as well.

Without dedicated and trained leadership,[6] any enterprise that involves more than two people will languish. There is need for clear leader-

---

4. Crabtree, *Empowering Church*, 54.

5. See also Stevens, *Liberating the Laity*, 26–42.

6. While it is beyond the scope of this book to explore the facets of leadership, there are many books on the market on leadership in general and leadership in the church. One of the most helpful for our time is Roxburgh and Romanuk, *Missional Leader*. I find their Three Zone model of leadership to be especially helpful. Most congregations are clearly in the "reactive" zone, which requires a particular kind of leader—one who asks questions and keeps people in conversation about the changes we are experiencing. In addition, Stevens and Collins, *Equipping Pastor*, has helpful information on leadership

ship if we are going to focus congregations on scattered ministries as well as gathered ministries. In this regard, there is one point that needs to be stated clearly, openly, and boldly: equipping the saints *begins* with the pastor and *permeates* the pastor's sense of call, or it doesn't stand a chance.

In the initial round of conversations, one pastor stated, "This all starts with our attitude—that we value what people do and we encourage their ministry." If pastors don't value what people do in the world, then nothing is going to change. If leaders can only speak in concrete terms about gathered ministries, and if they are unable to speak in concrete terms about scattered ministries, then any focus on the scattered church will remain a window dressing. In fact, if you are a pastor who is not convinced that congregations exist for the sake of mission[7], and that (in sheer volume) mission happens more in the day-to-day activities of members than it does in the programs of the congregation, then you might as well stop reading here. If you are a member of a church and your pastor does not share this perspective, then your work to introduce it is going to be significantly more difficult.

The same pastor who said that this starts with our attitude went on to add, "For instance, when someone cannot do something at church because of another commitment, we affirm the other commitment as their ministry right now and we find someone else to do what we need to have done." That is a clear example of the priesthood of all believers being at the center of a pastor's sense of ministry. Another pastor said, "My attitude is first; ministry in daily life is central to what I do." That pastor went on to offer an interesting mental image: "I find myself wanting to walk my people to the door. How do we shoo the people out and get the good news that we celebrate here into the community?" Indeed, how do we inspire and equip people to take the good news out of the building and speak and live it in the world? That is simple: the truth is it's already happening! We *have* been formed and shaped by our faith; the members in the forums (chapter 2) spoke to this clearly. Remember the person who said, "Ministry happens from the time you get up in the morning to when you go to bed."

In the early conversations with pastors I heard clearly that most of them *want* scattered ministries to be at the core of their ministry. There is no other way to explain the overwhelming interest they expressed in our

---

from a systems perspective. Chapter 8 has "ten principles for system equippers" and "ten ways to empower the laity for mission."

7. Nessan, *Beyond Maintenance*, xii.

conversations. Based on those same conversations, though, I know that many feel ill prepared to offer leadership in this area. Witness the pastor who said, "We (pastors) don't know about the ministries members are doing in the world." At the same time it's comforting to know that the wisdom to address this shortcoming exists among us. Searching for a way forward, one pastor said, "We need to train ourselves to see ministry in daily life before we can help lay people see it." In another of those early conversations, a pastor wisely said, "The teachers of ministry in daily life are the laity." Another added, "So pastors need to listen to the stories members are telling one another. We need to name the ministries members are doing. People do this casually . . ." and another finished the sentence, "but it helps when it's intentional. Those are powerful stories, and people will remember those more than my sermons." Pastors may feel ill prepared, but remember what Crabtree said earlier, "the laity [at my church] have done as much to equip me as I have to equip them." It takes a village.

In the anthology produced by people who were involved in a research project at Andover-Newton Theological Seminary on the ministry of the laity, the president of the seminary at the time describes his awakening to a vision of the church at work in the world, a vision that went far beyond anything that had occurred to him before. In the book's initial essay he wonders about the implications of several changes that would lift up the ministry of all Christians, but then he wonders in particular about his role as a pastor.

> What if I, as an ordained minister, now saw it as an absolutely basic, specific, explicit element in *my* ministry to provide resources for their ministry? What if I listened before I spoke? What if the whole church listened before it did anything—listened so as to learn what the ministry of outreach was all about, before the clergy tried to prescribe what the laity "needed"? What if, for its own upbuilding toward its mission, the church found ways to draw upon the rich store of understanding, insight, and expertise that is already there, but underutilized, in all of its members? . . . I wonder what would happen if the *laos* of God, all the people around the world, could speak with their varied voices and set forth their concerns. What, then, would be on the mind and in the programs of the church?[8]

When pastors make the ministry of their members an absolutely basic, specific, and explicit element of their own calls, ministry will multiply

---

8. Peck and Hoffman, *Laity in Ministry*, 17, 19. Emphasis in original.

beyond all expectations. When congregational leaders listen before they speak, they will hear stories of ministry that are powerful and compelling. When congregations draw on the rich store of understanding, insight, and expertise that is already present in their members, pastors—to their relief—will no longer be the primary person responsible for applying faith to life. When the *laos* of God utter their hopes and concerns for family members, work issues, and community concerns, the priorities and the programs of congregations will be focused on the many relevant, exciting, and compelling ways in which God is at work in the world—through all believers.[9]

CREATING AN EQUIPPING COMMUNITY

Being convinced of the promise of the scattered church is not the only role for the pastor and other leaders in the congregation. Equipping the saints begins with leaders, but the equipping happens in and among the Body. In order for the Body to do that work, leaders need to build and communicate a pervasive sense that our time as the gathered church is about preparing and empowering us to be the scattered church.

Having said that, we need to be careful. When we talk about leadership, most of us are trained to think first and foremost about adding on activities and programs. When evangelism rises up as a critical need, we look for Bible studies that we can offer, or we schedule an Invite A Friend Sunday. When stewardship becomes a pressing need, we look for the best method for eliciting contributions. The critical point here is that creating an equipping community is *not* simply a matter of adding more programs to our already busy slate of activities and emphases.

In a *Christian Century* article, Adam McHugh writes about various understandings of the nature of leadership. His final example cites Wilfred Drath and Charles Palus at the Center for Creative Leadership who say "most existing theories, models and definitions of leadership proceed from the assumption that somehow leadership is about getting people to do something." That is probably the predominant mode of leadership that church leaders are trained for. Drath and Palus invite us to reimagine leadership as "the process for making sense of what people are doing together so that people will understand and be committed." Based on what we have found about shaping a congregation around scattered ministries, this

9. See Prentiss and Lowe, *Radical Sending*, 81–94, for first-person stories of leaders who have worked to create equipping congregations.

alternate view of leadership is both appropriate and encouraging. McHugh concludes:

> Leadership, in this view, is a matter of providing interpretation. Leaders give people a lens and a language for understanding their work and experiences in light of larger purposes. They help shape the mental frameworks of others so that those people see themselves as making contributions to the mission and direction of their organization, working in community for a common purpose.[10]

IT HAS TO BE CENTRAL

Just as the call to equip the saints needs to permeate the pastor's sense of call, so it needs to permeate the gathered community's sense of purpose. In fact, and to state this bluntly and clearly, *the ministry of the saints in the world needs to be central to everything that the congregation is and does.* If it's not, then something else will be at the center. Based on earlier chapters, we know that *something else* will likely be an inward focus on the gathered church's health and vitality.

Consider my story as an example. Over the years in my parish ministry, those seminary memories I spoke of earlier would come to mind. Sometimes they spurred me to make an effort to demonstrate that scattered ministries are important. The method I chose on several occasions was to affirm the ministry of our members in Sunday worship.

In my last congregation, I worked with staff to set up a monthly recognition of members, grouped by job types. The first month of the emphasis fell in September, so it was a natural fit to affirm teachers and students. We called all educators and students forward and commissioned them for their ministry. Living in a community that had a large teaching hospital, we decided that October would focus on health professionals. By the time November came around, well, Advent and Christmas were staring us in the face and we got sidetracked. By the time we recovered from Christmas, Lent was looming, then Easter, and before we knew it another program year had flown by and our determination to celebrate the ministries of our people and commission them for that work had long since faded.

---

10. McHugh, "Can introverts lead?," final paragraph.

Two things are obvious now, looking back on that experience. First, we approached this emphasis as a stand-alone activity. It was the proverbial icing on the cake for a congregation that was juggling a lot of programs. Because of that, our best intentions were undone by the relentless drumbeat of the program year. Other things *had* to be done, so this optional emphasis fell by the wayside. Second, we launched this attempt at affirmation unannounced and without any context or rationale—outside of a sermon that addressed ministry in the world. Is it any wonder, then, that people came forward to be affirmed and commissioned with puzzled looks on their faces? Is it any wonder that the promises they made were half-hearted and forgotten before their Sunday dinner was done?

Other congregations have made good faith attempts at communicating the message of ministry in the world to their members. Many of the attempts are in the form of signage and slogans. The most common technique I've seen to communicate the fact that ministry does not belong just to the pastor(s) is a listing of church staff that begins, "The people of First Church, ministers," and then goes on to list the pastors, musicians, and other staff. Perhaps you, too, have seen signs posted at the exit to the building that read, "You are now entering the mission field." I was intrigued to drive past one church that posted a sign at the beginning of the driveway that reads, "Enter to worship." A few hundred feet down the street, at the exit from the parking lot, a similar sign reads, "Exit to serve."

These are all encouraging indicators that we are already aware of the gathered and scattered nature of the church. But if these attempts to communicate are not part of an overall understanding that our gathering serves to equip, empower, and send our people into the world, they will fall short. If the signs and slogans are not backed up by intentional, constant, pervasive, and concrete explanation and exploration of what scattered ministries look like, they will not make a significant difference in the life of our congregations.

Equipping the saints for ministry in the world is not one program of the church among many. It is not work that is assigned to a few people while everybody else works in other areas. It is not an optional activity that we add on to everything else—*if* we have the time and energy. The underlying assumption of this book is that equipping the saints for ministry is the central work of the church.

Norma Cook Everist and Nelvin Vos say this well. In speaking of the temptation to add on programs and activities that work for the purpose of equipping the saints—important and appropriate as those activities might be—they say:

> [T]he most crucial element to help members connect faith and daily life is to have this mission *permeate* every program and activity of the congregation. Rather than seeing ministry in daily life as a separate and isolated understanding, approach and evaluate and *connect* every aspect of congregational life with the question: How will this support members to be ambassadors for Christ in their daily lives? Does our worship lead to such a response? Is our educational program equipping people to be disciples? Does our understanding and practice of stewardship help people to see that their lives are the most important gift to be given back to God? Only by really probing such questions will the challenge of being a church in mission in the world become the *bloodstream* of the congregation.[11]

Everest and Vos raise important questions about the interrelatedness of gathered and scattered ministries. We will return to them in the next chapter.

MAKING THE SHIFT

Imagining and creating an equipping environment, in one sense, need not be as difficult as it might sound. Leaders can start by providing time for people to articulate the ministry that they are already doing. Considering that most of us are not accustomed to doing this, leaders can model the desired behavior by attending to and naming the ministry we see and hear from our members. As one pastor said, "It's not a program to teach them how to do ministry; it's a matter of helping them see that they are doing ministry."

Davida Foy Crabtree describes this role well:

> My job as an ordained leader is not to do the equipping of the individuals (though in some cases I must), but to build up the community in such a way that the community empowers itself by its living as the Body of Christ, by its explicit acts of training and teaching. . . .
>
> [T]he role of the ordained minister is to build community in such a way that it embodies and empowers the mission and

---

11. Everist and Vos, *Where in the World*, 126–7. Emphasis in original.

ministry of all God's people in and to the world. I am not the em-
powerer. The Holy Spirit, which infuses the Body of Christ with
vitality and power, does the empowering of the faith community.[12]

It might be helpful to look at this as a matter of choice. As a congregational leader, which would you rather spend your time on: prying out bits
and pieces of members' time, energy, and resources to support an activity
of the congregation, or talking with people about the many things they are
already doing that support God's dream, and then supporting and empowering them to do those things?

On the other hand, we need to address the reality that creating an
empowering community is a challenging undertaking. Such work requires
decoding the DNA of the congregation and the behaviors that it drives.
This task is not simple, but investing the time to create an empowering
community will provide the whole people of God with an understanding and experience of ministry in the world that will be both relevant and
life-giving.

PAYING ATTENTION TO THE SYSTEM
—AND THE CULTURE

In the previous section, Crabtree described the work of an ordained leader
in terms of building up the community in such a way that the community
empowers itself. What I haven't yet revealed is that the whole of her book is
focused on the question of aligning the structure of the congregation with
the purpose of equipping people for ministry. Crabtree explains:

> Part of my responsibility as an ordained person in the role of
> equipping the saints is to clarify and interpret the structures and
> systems which shape the life of the community of faith. I do not do
> it alone, but always (as with everything in ministry) in the midst
> of that community.[13]

Crabtree tells the story of how her congregation sought to "empower
the ministry of the laity in their daily lives." The book opens with the discovery that their preaching and programming to strengthen the ministry
of the laity were contradicted by organizational systems and structures that

---

12. Crabtree, *Empowering Church*, 34–35.

13. Ibid., 35.

focused on "holding-them-here" rather than "sending-them-out."[14] Acknowledging that form does not always follow function, her book reports on the work she led to realign both the expectations and the structure of the congregation so that it would empower people for their work in the world, rather than block it.

As we saw in chapter 2, pastors are aware of the systemic blocks that stymie work on scattered ministries. The fact that there are systemic blocks really shouldn't come as a surprise. Something as inadvertently foreign as the priesthood of all believers is not going to be (re)introduced to a congregation without paying attention to both the visible and the hidden characteristics that determine a congregation's behavior.

A good many books on the market[15] describe congregational characteristics in terms of *culture* and *systems*. In short, *systems* offer a description of the way we are structured, in an effort to fulfill that which we hope to do. The *culture* of a congregation, on the other hand, is a description of what we actually do and expect. Mallory helpfully says, "Systems can often be analyzed from the outside; cultures must be understood from the inside."[16] Systems are usually overt and easy to identify: most congregations can easily describe their organizational chart consisting of a council or a vestry at the top, various boards or committees, and staff persons assigned particular tasks. New pastors who want to discuss plans for worship know to turn to the worship committee and music staff. Members who want to talk about the condition of the carpet know to go to the property committee.

Cultures, on the other hand, are often covert and not as easy to identify; pastors new to a congregation (and I'm speaking from experience here) often don't discover the expectations and responsibilities that are shaped by the congregation's culture until they violate or fail to meet them. "It would have been nice if someone had told me," is my usual thought when I step on one of those culture-driven land mines. Taking a vote at a congregational meeting might be a good way to change the *system*; a congregational vote is likely to have little impact on the underlying *culture*.

The important point here is that it is difficult to bring about change without first understanding both the congregation's culture and its system.

14. Ibid., ix.

15. Three books that I read in the first few months of this journey (Mallory, *Equipping Church*; Crabtree, *Empowering Church*; and Stevens and Collins, *Equipping Pastor*) are built around systems theory. If you're not familiar with the theory, you can read about it in any of these three and many other books.

16. Mallory, *Equipping Church*, 54.

Only after considerable work has been done to bring these dynamics into the open can leaders speak to and shape the culture, and then realign the system to support new goals and purposes.[17] Mallory speaks to their inter-relatedness:

> Though systems and culture are not identical, they must work in harmony. When they cooperate and support one another, healthy growth, positive change, and transformed lives are all possible. . . .
> I can't emphasize enough how pointless it is to change a system and not address its underlying culture. The converse is true as well: you can't simply make changes in the culture without attending to the systems it drives.[18]

Stevens and Collins add another helpful insight from systems theory: "It is difficult if not impossible to change individuals directly without changing the system."[19] Later in the book, in talking about creating an "equipping environment," they talk about the power of the system if left unchecked:

> A pastor may facilitate a training program of lay pastoral care giving, but if the environment communicates that only a professional can be of any help, the program is undone by the environment. The problem is systemic. A pastor may equip Christians to discover their ministry in the workplace, but if the structures and ethos of the church "eat up" people's time in housekeeping and maintenance tasks, equipping for *diaspora* [the scattered church] is frustrated. A lay leader may start a discipleship training program, but if the relationships in the church are impersonal and functional, the training program is at odds with the systemic reality of the church. A pastor may start a lay evangelism program, but if new Christians are frozen out of the church by lovelessness or driven out by [hypocrisy] . . . The problem is not programmatic but systemic.[20]

The fact that pastors can identify systemic blocks to creating an equipping congregation is encouraging. Knowing what threatens to block leadership in this area is a necessary first step. Being willing and able to discuss

---

17. See Stevens, *Liberating the Laity*, 73–74 for a good, brief series of steps for facilitating structural change.

18. Mallory, *Equipping Church*, 54–55.

19. Stevens and Collins, *Equipping Pastor*, xix.

20. Ibid., 46.

openly and non-anxiously both the culture and the system is an important second step. It is only after awareness has been raised about the pressures and the purposes of both overt structure and hidden assumptions that leaders can begin to compare and imagine alternative objectives and paths.[21]

Stevens and Collins affirm the message of this chapter in two sentences:

> The most direct way to equip the saints for the work of the ministry is not to devise strategies for equipping individuals but to equip the church (as a system). Then the church will equip the saints.[22]

While equipping the saints for ministry has to be central to the pastor's sense of call, equipping is not just the work of the pastor. It's not just the job for a committee. It belongs to the whole Body.

Given that, let's take a look at what an equipping congregation might look like.

---

21. See Stevens, *Liberating the Laity*, 53, for two good points on this work: 1) structures should be participational rather than representative (e.g., rather than letting the best teacher teach, get as many people to participate as possible), and 2) structures should be relational rather than organizational.

22. Stevens and Collins, *Equipping Pastor*, 41.

8

From Imagination to Reality

My wife was a constant companion through the journey of conversation and discovery described in this book. She was my notetaker in the forums. She participated in conversations when the subject came up with friends. After several years of enduring my fixation on this topic, she finally asked me, *So what would an example of a thriving church built on the principles of scattered ministries look like?*

The answer may be surprising: A congregation built around and structured for scattered ministries would probably not look a lot different than what we now know. Worship would still be at the center. Faith formation would continue to be critically important. Pastoral care would still be offered. A strong sense of community among the members would be as important as ever. In short, much of what we have been doing as the gathered church continues to be vital, even when the scattered ministries of all God's people are central to our gathering.

So what would be different? If we make the scattered church as important as the gathered church, priorities will shift, we will let go of some traditional ways of being and doing, some of what we are currently doing will be reimagined, and new approaches will be given room to take root. This chapter proposes some initial ideas about what those changes and new approaches might look like.

MAKING ROOM FOR SCATTERED MINISTRIES

The house my wife and I live in is blessed with a yard full of mature trees. The trees provide a wonderful canopy of shade. It is a joy to be able to go out in the yard without being overwhelmed by the summer sun. The drawback is that it is difficult to grow grass, flowers, and bushes, and a vegetable garden is out of the question. Hostas do well, but that's about it. We also have a lovely cedar tree outside our kitchen. An arborist informed us that it was dying because the surrounding trees were competing for the light it needs. We wound up cutting down several trees around it, much to our chagrin, but to the cedar tree's delight. To our delight, an area near the cedar tree—where several attempts to grow grass had failed dismally—started growing lush grass.

Likewise, it is possible that the canopy of mature programs and activities in our congregations is overshadowing that which God is calling us to be and do in the world. It might be that a "tree" or two needs to come down in order to provide the space and the light for new ways of being and doing to thrive. Like the grass springing up next to our cedar tree, we might be surprised by the new life that erupts when we let light penetrate where it has not before.

Re-forming a congregation around the principles of both gathering and scattering will be a matter of making room amid our gathered ministries so that scattered ministries have room to thrive. We will need to set our persistent focus on the vitality of the gathered church to the side, at least for the time being, so that we are open to the development of new ways of seeing and supporting ministry. My assumption—and my hope—is that when the gathered church focuses on the multitude of ways that we are already serving in God's name when we are scattered, we will find new and surprising life, meaning, vitality, and joy in our gathering.

Leaders who want to balance the gathered and scattered nature of the church will engage in extended and ongoing conversation about all that we do as a gathered community of faith and why we do what we do.[1] We will ask intentional questions about how those activities either support or block efforts to equip and empower people to serve God's purposes in the world. Some questions will raise awareness of that which no longer serves us well and needs to be left behind, others will reveal that which is still helpful and

---

1. See the excellent discussion of leadership in the reactive zone where such conversation is required in Roxburgh and Romanuk, *Missional Leader*, especially chapter 5 and following.

can be brought along on the journey, while still others will lead to new ideas and opportunities.

Making room for questions and conversation about what we have been doing, are doing, and want to do will be one of the first changes in a congregation that wants to focus on the scattering. Only after this work is done can we begin to imagine experiments that might be worth trying. Only then will we be able to bring both the culture and the structure of the congregation into alignment with God's intentions that we would be a blessing to the world (Gen 12:1–3).

As we work to open this space so that we can bring the culture and the structure of the congregation into alignment with the principles of the scattered church, a word of caution is in order. If you're like me, you're likely to read some of the ideas that follow and think, "I've tried that before." Like me, you may add, ". . . and it never really made much of a difference."

I remind you of what I said in chapter 7: *the ministry of the saints in the world needs to be central to everything that the congregation is and does.* If it's not, then something else will be at the center. For that reason, questions and conversation about gathered church programs and assumptions that might override any focus on scattered ministries will be as important as any other discussion we can have. Clearing out the overgrowth so that light can penetrate will be vital in order for the following ideas to take root.

TALKING IN CONCRETE TERMS

Congregations need to learn how to talk about scattered ministries openly and concretely. Members are already talking concretely about their lives in private conversations and small groups. When we gather in fellowship, we talk about our work, families, volunteer activities, and recreational pursuits. The problem is that we are not trained to talk about these activities as the means by which God is at work through us for the welfare of our neighbors.

A congregation built on the principles of the scattered church will affirm much of what all of God's people (including pastors) are doing as parents, workers, citizens, and friends as ministry. Those who feel burdened by being in the sandwich generation (both raising children and caring for older parents) will not only be encouraged, but their caregiving will be lifted up as a vital ministry. God's presence in the care they provide will be celebrated, and they will receive prayer support and resources as needed. Congregations will name the way insurance agents provide support and security for others and commission them for that work. Students, whose vocation is learning, will be affirmed, and mentors will teach them how to view their education and their gifts as a blessing to all people and all creation. Everyone will be taught to see connections between stories in the Bible and the stories of our lives. Again, it's not so much a matter of adding something to what we are already doing; it's more a matter of shifting our thinking, our teaching and preaching, our life together in community, and our conversation so that the scattering is as important as the gathering.

CONNECTING WORSHIP AND THE WORLD

A congregation based on the principles of the scattered church will make the critical connection between what we do in worship and what we do in the world. As we have seen, references to ministry in and to the world are abundant in our liturgies, hymnody, Scripture readings, sermons, and prayers—but often only in generic terms. One of the most significant challenges in reimagining worship will be to turn generic language (e.g., "strive for justice") into concrete realities *in terms of our scattered ministries.*

How does worship support us to be ambassadors for Christ in our daily lives? How can we shape worship so that it compels us to reflect on our lives, the times where we failed to be God's people, the instances where we see God at work in the world, as well as the places where we are called to be God's people at work? This section looks at some of the typical components of worship and how we might strengthen them so that we are overtly and concretely equipped to go in peace to serve the Lord.

Gathering liturgies

When we gather we will designate time to check in with one another, and we will use the time of confession and forgiveness to lift burdens from those who feel they have failed to be God's people at work in their daily interactions. Reimagining the gathering liturgies, especially confession and forgiveness, in concrete, scattered ministry terms, has the potential of being powerful. As it is now, we send everyone out at the end of worship, but when we re-gather we rarely ask, "How did it go last week?" In so doing, we are undermining the importance of the sending. It's like a boss who assigns a weekly task, but never checks to see if the employee does the work.

Sooner or later the employee will realize that the work is unimportant and stop doing it.

Holding people accountable to their calling is as important as equipping them for their calling, so we could ask questions like, "Where did you join in God's work in the world this week?" or "In what moment or relationship did you look the other way when sharing God's love was possible?" We will offer forgiveness for such failings and pray for strength to do better next time.

I recently had the opportunity to try an experiment along these lines. I prepared a "Checking In" handout that listed words and phrases from the prior Sunday's liturgy, hymns, and sermon that called us to love or serve others.[2] At the beginning of worship I gave the people time to review the list and then to write down instances where they had seen those words and phrases come to life in the past week, or where they had failed to do what they had been sent to do. After a few minutes of reading and reflection, I asked the people to share one item on their list with someone sitting nearby.

While the people were reflecting on the list, I sat down and read the list myself. One prayer in the list popped out; I realized that I had an opportunity to provide testimony to the resurrection when a relative of one of our family members died during the week—and I had failed to do that. The opening confession and forgiveness that followed this exercise was meaningful for me in a way that it hadn't been for a long time.

The exercise was as meaningful for others as it was for me. After three weeks of using the Checking In exercise, I asked the congregation to evaluate it. The results were extraordinary. The people were almost unanimously appreciative of the exercise. Eighty-three percent of them thought we should do something like this again, maybe even on a regular basis. Eighty percent reported becoming much more aware of the words we speak or sing in worship and how they are connected to daily life. While half of the respondents reported at least some ability to connect worship with daily life before the experiment, 72 percent said that the experiment made it easier for them to make that connection. One person suggested that a midweek email that recapped Sunday's worship could help people make the connection. It was a simple experiment, but it had a significant impact on our life together, and it definitely equipped the people to live into their scattered ministries.

2. A sample is available at www.TheScattering.org.

language

Preaching

I won't attempt to provide a comprehensive examination of how to preach to equip the saints for the work of ministry, but preaching needs to be included in this list of connections between worship and the world. We can take comfort in the assurance that connections between faith and life are already present in many, if not most, sermons. Again, this is something that we don't need to add to what we're already doing. We might, however, want to revisit how we're doing it.

Over the course of this project I began to assume that I had not done a good job in the past of connecting faith and life in my sermons. Late in the journey, I began working as an interim pastor. Being back in the pulpit gave me the opportunity to look over old sermons. I was surprised by how often and persistently I had made the connection. Quite often, though, my preaching fell victim to the lack of concrete examples. In this most recent experience of preaching, it's been a considerable challenge for me to make the connection between faith and life more specific.

In his book *Preaching at the Crossroads*, David Lose offers a very helpful and relevant chapter called "Preaching the Grandeur of God in the Everyday."[3] Lose describes the disconnect between Sunday and Monday, offers a very helpful and concise summary of vocation, and says, "I believe that the Sunday sermon is a principal place from which to lend our people the conviction that, seen from the perspective of baptismal faith, there is no small or meaningless gesture, and that what we sometimes think of as 'mundane' or 'ordinary' or even 'secular' life is simply bursting with the possibility for meaning and purpose."[4] Perhaps the most helpful part of this chapter is his suggestion of preaching to the "middle zone" of our lives. "Most of the illustrations I hear," he writes, "are directed to one of two zones or spheres of our life in this world. The first is the *congregational zone*." Readers of this book will recognize that zone immediately. "The second sphere . . . is what I'd call the *global zone*. Here the preacher takes up the matters of wars, natural disasters, global challenges" and the like. While he affirms that both of those zones are important, he adds, "what often seems to be missing are all those things that constitute our lives in between our congregational involvement and the world's very real problems. As it turns out, this is *most of our lives*." Lose then advocates preaching to the "middle

---

3. Lose, *Preaching at the Crossroads*, 65–78.

4. Ibid., 67.

zone," that is, the everyday elements of our lives. Supporting the premise of this book, Lose concludes, "Over time, through this and other practices your congregation may grow from being a place *where the word is preached* more fully into a *community of the word* where all the members take some responsibility for sharing the news of God's ongoing work to love, bless, and save the world."[5] Those who are charged with the task of preaching would do well to read Lose's book.

I can now attest to the difference that preaching with scattered ministries at the center can make. Just as this book was going through its final edits, I had the opportunity to preach on the same passage that yielded the word cloud in chapter 2. I used the same basic technique, wanting to see how the results might compare in a different setting. The results were almost identical; people listed family, busyness, and work as things that keep them from being God's people at work in the world.

On my way to preach that day, I realized that my approach was limiting; asking what keeps us from serving others will yield obstacles and stumbling blocks. In the car that morning I decided to add a second step to the sermon. After the people posted their sticky notes in the chancel, I reported the results I had found in my earlier sermon and the similar results they had just offered. I told them that many of the things we see as blocking us from ministering in God's name (e.g., family responsibilities, work, busyness) are the very ways that God calls us to ministry. I then affirmed caring for elderly parents, going to work, and being a citizen as ministry. Following that, I handed out new sticky notes and had them write down ways that they *are* God's people at work in the world. The responses were wonderfully encouraging. "Listening to others," "spending time with friends in need of comfort," "teaching my grandchildren," "praying for others," "telling others how God has carried me in my storms of life," "supporting my wife in her efforts," and "farming to feed people of the world" were among the many responses.

Testimony

One final finding from the Equipping Pastors conversations (chapter 2) introduces a rather unexpected way to connect worship to the world. Years ago I conducted a survey, looking for topics that would be of interest to potential workshop attendees. Participants were asked to rank twenty topics

---

5. Ibid., 75–77. Emphasis in original.

on two scales: 1) importance in the life of their congregation, and 2) the likelihood that people would attend a workshop on that topic. One of the topics was testimony and it scored so low on both scales that it was hard to graph it alongside the other topics. But in the original round of conversations with the pastors, I found a surprising and encouraging openness to the potential that testimony holds for the work at hand.

Some pastors revealed that they are using testimony; even more pastors indicated openness to trying it and awareness that it might be an appropriate way to equip the saints for the work of ministry. One pastor wondered aloud, "Is the disconnect between what we do at church and what people do in the world due to the fact that people are not hearing the stories of ministry from others?" Another said, "An equipping pastor helps people to identify and tell their stories of God at work in their lives. After the creed we have people tell their neighbor a story of where they've seen God at work this week." Another pastor reported hearing about a congregation that uses video blogs to tell short stories of people at work, sharing them by email.

To be fully transparent, distrust and suspicion of testimony was present. Speaking to both the skepticism that mainline Christians feel about testimony and its potential, one participant said, "We're considering implementing testimony in worship. Our council admitted, though, that they are afraid to name God's presence outside the church. I'm encouraging people to reflect on and talk about where they've seen God at work in the last week. I'm scared of testimony, but until we speak to one another about God's presence and activity, we won't, we can't, do it in daily life."

In short, testimony is an exciting possibility for giving voice to the struggles and the hopes of our people. Leaving my last congregational call to work at the Center for Renewal prevented me from following through on a plan to give up preaching time in order to make room for testimony. I knew I would have to train a few people to do that, and to do it well, but my hope was that after a few people had blazed the trail, others would say, "I can do that!"

Lillian Daniel wrote *Tell It Like It Is*, an encouraging book about how testimony changed and revitalized the congregation she was serving. According to Daniel, United Church of Christ congregations are just as skeptical of testimony as any other mainline denomination. Her work, though, showed that it can have a powerful impact on congregations that desire to turn their focus outward.[6]

In *Reclaiming the "C" Word*, Kelly Fryer briefly describes a "preaching and presiding team" of the pastor and five lay people who are, together, responsible for leading Sunday morning worship. It's her way of "setting people free" when we are the gathered church so we can minister "out there." She tells about Al, who is in the construction business, smokes cigars, and has a family with three children. "Nobody would probably ever say it out loud, but you know Al is the best preacher in the congregation." She also says that "when he preaches the sermon, every single person sitting there is thinking, 'Hey, if [Al] can talk about Jesus, why can't I?' "[7] Fryer's idea may sound radical to people who are accustomed to worship in which the pastor is the primary actor, but perhaps the idea of sharing responsibility for these tasks is one way of bringing daily life experiences into worship, and empowering scattered ministers for their scattered ministries.

A word of caution about testimony is in order: In keeping with the earlier observation about our tendency to focus mostly on matters related to the gathered church, the early conversations with pastors also revealed that testimony is often redirected from reflecting on God's activity in daily life to "how this congregation has helped me." This frequently happens at stewardship time when leaders are trying to help members see the value of contributing to the church. From what we have heard so far we know that it will take intentional training on the part of both leaders and members to focus on God's work *in the world* before testimony will become a transformative part of our life together.

Praying for the world

Another component of worship that could easily be reshaped to support our scattered ministries is the prayers. This is not a matter of reinventing the wheel; it is simply a matter of making the prayers more concrete. Instead of simply praying for "peace among nations," pray for peace in the specific areas of conflict that are in the news that week. Instead of praying for "food for the hungry," pray for the local food bank or soup kitchen, pray for farmers who grow it (name them if they are in your congregation),

---

6. See also Long, *Testimony*, chapter 3, "Sunday Words," for a strong connection between Sunday and Monday.

7. Fryer, *Reclaiming*, 69–72.

and pray for parents who will go home to feed their children, naming such activities as ministry. Instead of praying for "justice and equality," pray for news stories that week that have to do with fair and sustainable wages, for members if they are headed to the polls that week, and for those who work in legal professions or at city hall. If there is a way to involve the people in the task of preparing the prayers for worship, all the better; that is a great way to make the connection between worship and the world.

Tom Nelson, pastor of an Evangelical Free congregation, has worked to embed an understanding of faith at work in his congregation. He included this paragraph in one of his pastoral prayers:

> Holy Spirit, empower us for honoring you and serving others in and through our various vocations at home, at school and in the marketplace. Grant us wisdom and strength in the work you have called us to do, whether that is taking a test in a classroom at school, participating in meetings at the office, serving customers on the phone or preparing a meal in the kitchen of our home. May the work of our hands be a sweet aroma of worship to you Lord.[8]

That is a great example of a prayer that expresses our daily ministries in concrete terms. As a result of working to make the connection between faith and life, Nelson reports that people say things like, "I have always felt like a second class citizen before," or, "Pastor, thanks for telling me my work really matters."[9]

Sending rites

If you are part of a tradition that has a sending rite at the end of worship, beef it up so that it is the true culmination of worship. Instead of just saying, "Go in peace; serve the Lord" (or one of the many variations), see what you can do to make that rite more concrete. If your worship order does not have a sending, look at what could be done to build on the benediction. It could be as simple as slipping in a sentence like, "You have been forgiven and fed, you have heard words of promise and hope, you have been supported and encouraged in community. Now go and share that forgiveness, that hope, and that encouragement with your friends, your family, and your coworkers." If the sermon had a theme, promise, or challenge connected to

8. Nelson, "Pastoral Prayer," para. 3. Nelson is the senior pastor of Christ Community Church in Kansas City. He is the author of *Work Matters*.

9. Armstrong, "Tom Nelson," para. 3.

scattered ministries, reprise the sermon in a sentence and tie it to the sending or benediction. Remember the pastor (chapter 7) who wanted to find a way to shoo the members out to share the good news that we celebrate in the community? This would be a way to do that!

If you have built equipping and empowering of members into small groups or classes, the sending would be the appropriate time to do a commissioning service for people who have been discerning their calling to ministry in the world.[10] I heard of a pastor who developed a rite of blessing people's hands by anointing their hands with oil, asking God to use their hands in service to others in everyday life. A friend of mine reworked the sending rite to involve children. Each week the children are asked to place their hands on the heads of an adult and to commission them for the ministry they will perform in the coming week. It would be helpful as well to spend time discerning the call that children have to be loving, to play cooperatively, to learn or to contribute to the welfare of their family, and to commission them as well.

There are other ways that worship could be reworked so that it builds bridges between the gathered church and the scattered church.[11] Just put on your scattered ministries glasses and look at what you are doing now, and other ways to weave our scattered ministries into worship will become apparent to the attentive observer.

REIMAGINING FAITH FORMATION

Repeatedly over the course of this project I have bumped up against a basic truth: many of us find it difficult to think and talk about our scattered ministries. I suspect this is because of how the gathered community has formed and shaped us: We have been conditioned to see God on Sunday, in worship. Bible study is seen more as a matter of knowing facts about the Bible than it is about how to apply the Bible to life. We have not always done our best to equip people to see God in the world.

The fact that we find it difficult to think and talk about our scattered ministries calls for better and more appropriate ways of approaching faith formation. I am grateful our language has shifted in recent years from

---

10. Lutherans should take advantage of and build on the "Affirmation of Christian Vocation" on page 84 of *ELW*.

11. See Diehl, *Ministry in Daily Life*, 22–32 for additional ideas for making the connection in worship.

Christian education to *faith formation*. The gathered community is not so much about educating people (that is, teaching information); it is about forming faith. The Christian faith is not a body of doctrines to be learned, a set of Bible verses to be memorized, or a list of rules to be followed. Faith is a way of life that is formed in community through a lifetime of finding God in the midst of real, daily life experiences.

All of God's people need to be formed so that we can simply and naturally talk about faith to one another. If we can't do that when we gather, we will certainly not be able to do it when we scatter. We all need exposure to the Bible in a way that makes a direct connection between the people in the Bible and our own lives; we need the ability to identify our story in the Bible's stories and to identify the Bible's story in our story. We need to be able to theologize, that is, we need to be formed so that we see the holy in the mundane. Leaders do not necessarily need to set up new classes in order to accomplish this—which would require people to devote more time to the church. Rather, start with existing opportunities like devotions at committee meetings; introduce a passage and then engage in conversation about the passage. Use existing small groups—whether they are focused on relationship and Bible study, or whether they are focused on a task—to engage people in one-on-one conversation about faith and life. Allow a few minutes of one-on-one conversation between worshipers during the sermon. And, of course, shift the focus of existing classes and forums so that day-to-day application of any passage or topic is included.

When you introduce thoughtful reflection on the intersection of scripture and our daily lives, be ready to set an example as this is likely to be a foreign experience for many. Think through how you would respond if you were in a group and someone asked you the questions you're preparing to ask, and if others have a hard time answering be prepared to model the kind of response you're hoping for. Ask, listen, prod, and ponder along with those gathered—giving everyone the power to interpret and apply. Coming across as the expert, while it's helpful in some situations, can disempower rather than equip people when we're talking about applying faith to life.

THE POWER OF SPIRITUAL PRACTICES

Forrest's story in the Interlude pointed to the power and the importance of spiritual practices. During the time he was discerning whether God was calling him to begin a new business or commit to full-time ministry,

Forrest kept a journal. He engaged regularly in prayer. He sought advice from Christian friends and colleagues. Spiritual practices such as these are helpful tools for those who seek to connect faith with daily life.

Spiritual practices are the time-honored activities of the church by which people are incorporated into, learn, and live out a new way of life. Spiritual practices include those things we do when we gather: prayer, study of scripture, eating together, greeting one another, singing together, supporting one another, and giving out of what we have received. In addition, and based on Jesus' example, practices include the scattered ministries of hospitality, doing justice, caring for creation, healing, invitation, and serving "the least of these" (Matthew 25:40). Taken as a whole, practices open us to God's presence and foster a deep connection with God's will, both for our individual lives and for the world around us.

Practices can be engaged individually, in contemplation, silence, and union with God. Practices also need to be taught, formed, and engaged in Christian community. Diana Butler Bass writes, "Practices imply practice, repetition, craft, habit, and art. . . . Practices possess standards of maturity and excellence to which practitioners can aspire." She concludes, "Practice might not make perfect, but it does appear to make pilgrims."[12]

Christian practices will be vital to those who hope to open our people to God's presence in the world and equip them to embody God's dream in all they do and say. It is beyond the scope of this book to review all of the spiritual practices, much less to examine how they can be applied to the connection between faith and life. Thankfully there are many books and resources[13] that provide sound guidance for leaders who want to use spiritual practices to equip people to make a deeper connection between faith and life. One book in particular, though, could play a vital role in shifting the attention of the congregation to God's presence and God's will: Charles Olsen's *Transforming Church Boards*. Olsen's premise is that you cannot change a congregation without first transforming its council or vestry. His vision is that when you do that, it is life-giving.

> If [board] meetings and relationships are life giving rather than
> life draining, the board can become a model of community and

---

12. Bass, *Practicing Our Faith*, 66.

13. See Bass and Briehl, *On Our Way*, Bass, *Practicing Our Faith*, and Bass, *The Practicing Congregation*, for examples. The Evangelical Lutheran Church in America offers helpful resources at http://www.elca.org/Our-Work/Congregations-and-Synods/Faith-Practices.

ministry for the whole church. As I see it, the level of commitment in a congregation will not rise above that of the set apart leaders. The sense of community and care for one another will not rise above that of the consistory. The stewardship practices will not rise above those of the council. The prayer life will not rise above that of the board. The capacity to reflect biblically and theologically will not rise above that of the vestry. The willingness to take a prophetic position will not rise above those of the deacons. The hope and excitement for future of the church will not rise above that of the session.[14]

I had the opportunity to implement Olsen's vision in the last congregation I served. It was truly a remarkable process, and the transformation was life-giving for both the council and the congregation. If you want to introduce spiritual practices to your congregation, start with your managing board.

AN EXPERIMENT IN REFRAMING STEWARDSHIP AND EVANGELISM

What would happen if we reimagined stewardship and evangelism according to scattered church principles? Considering that some people call these two topics the "dirty words" of the church,[15] perhaps it's time to revisit them.

Recently I had the opportunity to do just that. I engaged thirty-three pastors from five denominations in two events for intentional conversation about stewardship and evangelism.[16] In chapter 7 I said that leadership in our time is a matter of asking questions and keeping people in conversation; these conversations proved the value of that methodology.

We talked about stewardship and evangelism separately, using a similar conversation guide for each. I first asked participants to work alone for a few minutes to establish a baseline definition of each topic. I told them that I expected they would write down legitimate, theologically valid definitions; I added that they had permission to list jaded, stereotypical definitions as well.

14. Olsen, *Transforming*, 9.

15. Reese, *Unbinding the Gospel*, 4, notes that a good many people call evangelism the "e-word." In conversation I heard someone else call stewardship the "f-word," that is, finances.

16. See www.TheScattering.org for a complete report on these conversations..

Signs of stress and pain were frequent in the baseline definitions of both topics. Stewardship was defined as "a matter of meeting the ministry plan that has been set by the church council in financial terms." More broadly, stewardship as we usually define it is concerned mostly with what we give to the church. The most common baseline definitions of evangelism revolved around inviting people to church, which (participants noted) is connected to bringing in new members. "More people," after all, "means more money," they said. Second, participants noted that evangelism is about sharing our faith, but there is considerable fear associated with that. Evangelism is stereotypically associated with street preaching, fire and brimstone, saving souls, or telling people how to get to heaven.

Despite my instructions to record solid theological or practical definitions, those were fairly rare in the baseline definitions. Looking back on these comments, I wonder if our persistent focus on the vitality of the gathered church is the driver of the many jaded responses. Do we somehow sense that our focus is on keeping our life, all while knowing that we are supposed to lose it for the sake of the world?

Signs of hope

When the conversations turned to scattered church alternatives, energy and hope abounded. Among the more frequent comments that emerged regarding stewardship were references to activities and programs that the church doesn't often give much attention to: community gardens, advocacy and political involvement, living simply, caring for friends and family, volunteering, citizenship, or donations to Goodwill. Two primary foci for a reimagined understanding of evangelism involved *speaking* and *living* the faith. Participants who defined evangelism in terms of speaking the faith noted the importance of building relationships with people, listening, and engaging in true dialogue. Those who spoke of living the faith mentioned living the good news of God's love in our daily activities and relationships. Participants said it's a matter of "being the church of Jesus Christ wherever we may be," or "interesting others in what motivates you by the way you act."

What was especially intriguing was that the legitimate, theologically valid definitions that I urged participants to write in their baseline definitions surfaced when we examined scattered church alternatives, even though I did not say anything about this. Stewardship was described as "the things God empowers me to do or live out." One person said it's "the willingness to risk what I have been given or my whole being." One participant offered a helpful comparison: In gathered church terms, stewardship is a matter of "managing time, talent and treasure—for the good of the whole church and its mission(s)." On the other hand, this person wrote that seen through scattered church lens, stewardship is a matter of "managing time, talent, and treasure—for the good of others."

Just as they had done with stewardship, several participants noted that evangelism is a spiritual practice that is supported by adult faith formation. One person noted simply that evangelism as a way of life is "an opportunity; an adventure." Another noted that evangelism is the flip side of stewardship: where stewardship is a matter of living life faithfully, evangelism is a matter of helping others see that their life is already in Christ.

Try this at home: imagine writing a sermon, preparing a lesson plan, or crafting a committee agenda with the positive definitions of stewardship or evangelism that came out of the second half of the conversations. If people are naturally inclined to respond negatively to these topics, how would their responses be different if we focused on them as day-to-day faith practices? If you are leading a committee in either of these areas, and you find it difficult to get others involved, try talking to others about the possibilities stewardship and evangelism hold when we look at them through a scattered church lens. One pastor used the results from the above conversations with a member who had been a very reluctant recruit to lead the stewardship committee. When this person saw stewardship in scattered church terms, the pastor said, his face lit up, his reluctance disappeared, and excitement burst out. "You mean stewardship can be about more than just supporting the church?" he asked. Imagine how different that congregation's stewardship programming might be in the coming year.

As I processed the conversations, I realized that I might have created an unintentional and false dichotomy. Clearly, both stewardship and evangelism have legitimate, theologically valid definitions and functions in the gathered church and in the scattered church. Doing things (such as an annual appeal or inviting people to worship or other activities) that support the ongoing health of the congregation is necessary and helpful. At the same time, though, the conversations showed that we have not fully thought through the application of these spiritual disciplines for our life in the world. The best part of the conversations was the experience of seeing the really exciting and encouraging ideas—and most of the energy—surfacing in the scattered church conversations. All it takes, it seems, is someone asking the right questions and keeping people in conversation.

CHANGING THE SYSTEM

Chapter 7 looked at the difference between cultures and systems. Paying attention to both is important, as we can't change one without changing the other. Much of what has been considered so far points to cultural issues (the assumptions and expectations that affect how we *actually* do things). Consideration of matters involving the system (e.g., organizational charts, constitutions and bylaws, and job descriptions) that describe what we *should* do is also needed.

One particular systemic practice that came up repeatedly over the course of this project had to do with *reporting*. Reports usually ask us to count something: Count the number of people in worship. Count the cost of staffing the program. Count the value of our buildings. It is vital that we realize that what we count is what we value. Some say that what you measure is what will grow;[17] if we count worship attendance, and if those numbers are trending down, then we assume that we should focus our efforts on getting more people to attend worship. In short, our priorities show up in the numbers we report. Put in visual form, the photo I took in a local church is the kind of reporting that I find to be not only unhelpful, but troubling.

Obviously, this picture is troubling because the numbers are falling. When I posted this on Facebook in regard to this topic, one person replied immediately (in mock horror), "OMG! WE'RE DYING! WE NEED SOME KIND OF GIMMICK!! REMEMBER THE GOOD OLD DAYS?!?! WE REALLY PACKED THEM IN THEN!! PASTOR, WHAT ARE YOU GOING TO DO ABOUT THIS?!"

REGISTER OF **ATTENDANCE & OFFERING**

ATTENDANCE TODAY	124
ATTENDANCE LAST SUNDAY	146
ATTENDANCE A YEAR AGO TODAY	172
AVG. ATTENDANCE LAST YEAR	187
NUMBER ON THE ROLL	632

Even if the numbers on the first and third lines of the register were reversed, showing sizable growth, this reporting technique is still problematic.

---

17. See McNeal, *Missional Renaissance*; the subtitle reveals his thesis that we need to change our counting and reporting practices.

It's focused on the gathered church. It shows that what we want and rejoice in is getting more people to attend church. Note well: There's nothing wrong with growth, in fact, any faithful person would and should rejoice in such a trend. But growth is a hoped-for result, not the objective of our life together. We don't exist to build bigger barns; the church exists to bless the world. So isn't that what we should count—isn't that what we should *value*? And if so, how might we shape reports so that we count and report what we value?

Try this at home: survey the committee, council (or vestry), and annual meeting reports in your congregation. Compile a list of what is counted, and by implication, what is valued. Pay attention to reports from the pastor. What do all the reports show to be important? What do the reports reveal about our (cultural) assumptions about where *ministry* is taking place? What systemic requirements do the reports meet, but in the process how do such reports overlook or denigrate our scattered ministries?

Once the list is compiled, engage others in conversation about the assumptions and practices that the reports reveal. (Use the chart at the end of chapter 2 to guide the conversation.) Ask questions about why we report what we report. List those things in the reports that have lost their usefulness. List those things that are not reported that should be included to more accurately reflect the importance of both the gathered and scattered church. From there, brainstorm ways that you might reshape the reports in your congregation, and in the process focus more on the ministry we all perform as God's scattered ministers.

The possibilities for rethinking our reporting system are endless. Breaking out of the box we have been in for a very long time might be difficult, even painful. Finding ways to change the reporting system, however, will be vital.

Let me offer a couple of ideas to stir your creativity. First, take the regular reports that are printed for your congregation's annual meeting (worship committee, property board, finance, etc.) and push them the back of the booklet, freeing up space in the front for stories from the lives of members. What might happen if examples of our scattered ministries were celebrated at the annual meeting? What might change if the traditional reports were evaluated based on how well the reporting group or activity supported our scattered ministries?

A second idea for reporting is related to the first. After one of the forums I led, one pastor rewrote his annual report. Using the broadest definition of the church as the people (the *ekklésia*, the called-out ones), this pastor based his report on what the people did in the world during the past year. Without naming names he described how the medical needs of many people had been met through the ministries of a doctor, a physician's assistant, and a large number of nurses from the congregation. He said the lives of many were enhanced through the work of engineers who make products that are safe and functional, and through those within the legal system who serve as police officers and lawyers, ministries that ensure safety and provide for the common good. He even lifted up the love, time, and energy shared with family, friends and community by those who are retired. Nearer the end of the report he described the functions of the church that are expected to be listed in such a report, but the impact of visits made, sermons preached, and meetings attended was set in a whole new light. He concluded by saying that "my report is a report of your ministry. And to each of you I add what Jesus says: well done, good and faithful servants."[18]

Finally, regarding reporting, a serious look needs to be given to the reporting expectations of denominations and judicatories. These larger systems will probably continue to want and need reports that focus on numbers, but they also need to look at other ways for congregations to report so that the focus expands to include what we do as the scattered church. In order to gather information from congregations about the ministry of all the baptized, judicatories will need to first teach, equip, and support congregations in their work of equipping all the baptized. At the very least, judicatory leaders would do well to give recognition to and support of the ministry of all the baptized, not just those who are ordained (and not just what the people do in or through the church).

In addition, *constitutional, budgetary, and programmatic priorities* in judicatories will need to be altered so that the ministry of all God's people is supported. In the constitution of our denomination, the chapter on ministry opens with this statement:

> This church affirms the universal priesthood of all its baptized members. In its function and its structure this church commits itself to the equipping and supporting of all its members for their ministries in the world and in this church. It is within this context

---

18. Mike Herschberger, Our Savior Lutheran Church, Marshalltown, IA. Used by permission. The full report is available on www.TheScattering.org.

of ministry that this church calls some of its baptized members for specific ministries in this church.[19]

While that is a strong value statement "supporting of all its members for their ministries," the actual practice is quite different. The next twenty-five pages of the constitution define what it means to be part of what we call the rostered ministries of the church (pastors, associates in ministry, deaconesses, and diaconal ministers). There is nothing in the constitution that defines or supports the ministries of the other 99.9 percent of the people. Budgets look similar. We provide budgeted support and programming for our gathered ministers and our gathered ministries; little is done for the rest. When judicatory constitutions, budgets, and programs center on the task of equipping the saints for the work of ministry, then they will be better prepared to request and celebrate reports that lift up the scattered ministers and scattered ministries of the church in addition to all that we do as the gathered church.

Another systemic practice that could be reimagined using a focus on scattered ministries is *job descriptions* and *evaluations.* In chapter 2 I listed the questions I asked at the lay forums about the possibilities of changing the job descriptions for pastors based on our conversation about ministry in daily life. Having had the conversation, the people said that equipping should be foremost in the job description. They said that we need to affirm the principle that the people do the ministry and the pastor supports what they do, not the other way around. How could we rewrite job descriptions so that staff members are not expected to do things that the rest of the congregation doesn't have the time to do, but are expected to equip the people for ministry—not just in the church but in the world as well? Job descriptions should at least include Ephesians 4:12; they could even be written with the task of equipping all the baptized as their core responsibility. Then, if job descriptions are paired with annual evaluations (as they should be) it would be possible to evaluate staff members not on the ministry they carried out on behalf of the members but in terms of how well they equipped others for ministry.

The systemic practice of *recruiting people for ministry* could also be reimagined. In the past, church leaders typically recruited people by way of a Time and Talent inventory. Reviewing whatever means your congregation uses to recruit people for ministry opportunities is likely to reveal both

---

19. Constitutions, Bylaws, and Continuing Resolutions of the Evangelical Lutheran Church in America, rev. April 2015, Chapter 7.11.

cultural assumptions and systemic expectations that are at work. Such surveys almost always list activities and opportunities that fall in the category of gathered ministries: teachers, committee members, food pantry workers, and worship leaders. What would it look like if we shaped these survey instruments so they include scattered ministries as well? Some readers might think, "We already do that. We recruit people to work at the shelter or to volunteer in a nursing home." That's good. I hope that's happening. But as we have seen, those activities lean more toward being gathered ministries. In addition, scattered ministries include many more things than volunteering. Scattered ministries include the whole of our lives as family members, workers, and citizens.

After one of the early Equipping Pastors conversations (chapter 2) in which I lifted up this possibility, a friend of mine took up the challenge. The fall stewardship campaign was approaching, and she used the opportunity to rework the Time and Talent sheets for the congregations she serves. Instead of typical categories like worship, education, and evangelism, she structured the inventory to follow our Affirmation of Baptism liturgy (e.g., proclaim the good news of God in Christ through word and deed; serve all people, following the example of Jesus; strive for justice and peace in all the earth[20]). Items like "steward the body God has given me through sufficient sleep, healthy eating, and adequate exercise" showed up along with "run the PowerPoint during worship." Other items included, "Pray for openness to the Holy Spirit's leading towards reconciliation when I am in disagreement with others," and "In my speaking, I will give God credit when credit is due to God." The usual gathered church opportunities were included, but as you can see, the list was expanded to affirm and support scattered ministries as well. The new Time and Talent sheets were introduced in a sermon based on parable Jesus told about the master who expected the servants to continue his business while he was gone (Matthew 25:14–30). "Your very life is what is at stake in this parable—for in God's grace you have received life and you are given responsibility for using the life God has given you to enlarge God's business of grace!"[21]

---

20. *ELW*, 237.

21. Virginia Anderson-Larson, St. John Lutheran Church, Olin, and Zion Lutheran Church, Wyoming, IA, November 13, 2011. Used by permission. The response form is available at www.TheScattering.org.

I COULD GO ON . . .

This chapter lists a few of the experiments and possibilities that I have come across in recent years that begin the work of getting us out of our gathered church box. I could go on. In fact, I trust I *will* go on to consider other ways that we can expand our thinking to empower and affirm scattered ministries as naturally as we do gathered ministries. By the time you read this book, I anticipate that I will have tried more experiments and come across more ideas for empowering a church that is committed to the scattering of God's people for acts of love and service. I will be posting those new developments to www.TheScattering.org. Come and see what else has come to light.

I hope and pray you will join the rethinking and the experimenting. The possibilities are as diverse as God's people are different. As you create and experiment, I hope you will post your work and your discoveries to www.TheScattering.org for others to see. Together we can not only imagine a church that connects faith and life, we can build communities that equip God's people for ministry both in the church and in the world.

Conclusion

The spiritual and social location of the church today is teeming with both challenges and opportunities. Maybe it's just the friends I keep and the news I read, but I constantly see posts and articles about the decline of the church, the irrelevance of the church, the stubbornness of the church, or predictions of the premature death of the church. There are several blog posts, for example, that compare Kodak to the church.[1] Describing how Kodak declined because it confused its product line with its mission, these posts caution that we should learn from Kodak's mistakes or risk the same fate. Given all this dire news, what should a good church leader do?

The wise move is to venture forth knowing that the fate of the church and of the world for which the church exists is not under our control, but is (and always has been) in God's hands. We might be witnessing changes that foretell the end of the church *as we have known it*, but I believe God's Spirit is at work in these changes to bring new life to both the church and the world. There is no reason for despair or discouragement—unless our only hope is to hold onto our Kodak moments. There is reason for hope and encouragement because God is constantly doing a new thing in our midst.

> Do not remember the former things, or consider the things of old.
> I am about to do a new thing; now it springs forth, do you not
> perceive it? I will make a way in the wilderness and rivers in the
> desert. (Isa 43:18–19)

We have no reason to think that the radical and unsettling change the church faces is unique to our day. The people of God have faced overwhelming odds as long as we have been God's people. Sometimes the pressure comes from external forces and sometimes it's from internal forces (just call

---

1. Type *kodak, church,* and *blog* into a search engine and you'll be treated to many examples.

to mind the people in the wilderness cursing Moses for rescuing them from slavery!); the passage from Isaiah 43 shows that sometimes change comes from God's creating and sustaining Spirit.

Douglas John Hall presents a definition of discipleship that fits hand-in-glove with the premise of this book: "*Discipleship of the crucified Christ is characterized by a faith that drives its adherents into the world with a relentlessness and daring they could not manage on the basis of human volition alone.*"[2]

If Hall is correct, and I think he is, the response to the changes we are experiencing is entirely counterintuitive: deny ourselves, ignore questions of institutional viability, and focus on that which all of us do in the world, in the roles, relationships, and responsibilities of our everyday lives.

I concur with John M. Buchanan who wrote in *The Christian Century*:

> I have a proposal: let's call a moratorium on counting members. Let's consider that we are called to witness to God's love in Jesus Christ and to do everything we can to be Christ's body in the world, to do what we believe he would be doing and is doing through us.[3]

This is no simple feat. Denying ourselves is hard. Denying our institutional selves might be even harder. But it is the way to life (see Matthew 16:24–26).

LOOKING BACK TO FIND THE WAY FORWARD

It may be that one difference in our day is that the new thing that God is doing among us is urging us to take a second look at an old thing. Not only can hope be found in reclaiming the promise of the gathered-scattered church, but it is an appropriate and timely answer to the growing hunger for meaning and purpose in our society.

If you search the Internet for "finding meaning and purpose in life" the result will be, literally, millions of hits. When I last did this search I found a fifteen-step process for finding meaning and purpose on Oprah's webpage, a five-step process on the Huffington Post, a blog post titled, "Fifteen Questions to Discover Your Personal Mission," and another post that promises, "How to Discover Your Life Purpose in About Twenty Minutes," to name

---

2. Hall, *Cross in Our Context*, 183. Emphasis in original.

3. Buchanan, "Being Christ's Body," 3.

just a few. Searching book retailers with the same phrase will yield books to help young adults find their path in life, and books to help the wave of retiring Boomers find meaning and purpose as they move beyond the daily grind. Indeed, there is a huge desire to find meaning and purpose in our lives. At the same time, though, we are told that people pay little to no attention to the church because we are cut off from the real world, answering questions that no one is asking, or simply serving as a burial society.

It doesn't take a crystal ball to see that the gathered/scattered nature of the church is a new/old thing that God is working in our midst. It not only offers the promise of making the church more relevant (an outcome that many church leaders attempt to achieve by changing the characteristics or programs of the gathered church), it offers the hope of a more meaningful and less stressful way of leading congregations.

Having made the journey described in this book, this is where I stand: If restoration of the ministry of all God's people is not the most important topic for congregational renewal, it's at least in the top three. Darrell Guder says our task is to guide people "to identify God's calling, to recognize the gifts and opportunities they have, to provide them the biblical and theological training to incarnate the gospel in their particular fields, and then to commission them to that ministry." A little later he says, "If a mission community saw itself primarily as the Spirit's steward of the calling and gifts of its members, its internal activities would, in one sense, diminish. It would spend much less time on providing activities that take its members out of the world." Then he adds, "Our concept of 'active church member' would, of course, have to change."[4]

My vision is of a community of believers that sees its purpose in terms of forming followers of Christ who are equipped and empowered to be his agents of love, care and compassion in the world. It is a vision of a community that gathers on a regular basis to hear reports from the front lines, and to engage the ancient practices of the church (scripture, worship, prayer) around matters of relationships, calling, and culture. It is a vision of a gathered community that earnestly discerns how God's presence influences what we do with our lives from Monday through Saturday, and then sends us back out into the world, in peace, to serve the Lord. This vision will expand our understanding and practice of *ministry* beyond our wildest expectations. This vision will make our congregations incredibly exciting and vibrant places. Living out this vision will finally provide an answer to

---

4. Guder, *Continuing Conversion*, 178–9.

the question, "Why are so many people leaving the church?" Why? Because they're heading back out into the world as God's agents of hope, faith, and compassion!

APPENDIX

Resources to Feed Your Imagination

ONLINE RESOURCES

The **Theology of Work Project** offers an extensive set of resources for connecting faith and work. (http://www.theologyofwork.org/key-topics/the-equipping-church) One of their more ambitious projects is to provide commentary on every passage in the Bible that relates to work. The work of the project can also be followed on Facebook (https://www.facebook.com/theologyofwork?fref=ts).

Redeemer Presbyterian Church in New York City has a **Center for Faith & Work** that emphasizes the importance of meaningful faith and work integration. http://www.redeemer.com/renew/center_for_faith_work

The High Calling offers a broad range of articles, interviews, devotionals, videos, and inspirational stories to help integrate faith with work, family, and the broader culture. http://www.thehighcalling.org

Connections is a free online resource offered by Wartburg Theological Seminary (Dubuque, Iowa). It explores how the creating, redeeming, and life-giving God is creating and redeeming today: in our homes, workplaces, neighborhoods, places of recreation, and volunteer activity. http://www.wartburgseminary.edu/resources/connections-resource-congregations

As this book was going to print, a grassroots effort in the Evangelical Lutheran Church in America called the **Life of Faith Initiative** was just beginning. The initiative's purpose is to stir up a culture change that frees the church to make the service of the baptized in the arenas of daily life the central focus of its mission. http://life-of-faith.org

Princeton Faith and Work Initiative does academic research and offers practical resources for the issues and opportunities surrounding faith and work. The Initiative explores pressing marketplace topics, including ethics, global competition and its ramifications, wealth creation and poverty, diversity and inclusion, conflicting stakeholder interests, and social responsibility. www.princeton.edu/faithandwork

Celebrate Your Work offers a free **Take Your Pastor to Lunch** invitation. The invitation reads, in part, "I would like to buy your lunch and discuss how to better minister in the area of influence in which God has placed me here at work." See the *Take Your Pastor to Lunch* tab, then click on the sample invitation. Celebrate Your Work offers links to several other faith at work groups on its webpage and offers other resources as well. http://celebrateyourwork.com

Faith@Work is a network for sharing ideas and resources that help bridge the gap between faith and the workplace. http://www.faith-at-work. net

Select Learning offers good resources on many topics. In their *Christian Life* category, three titles are especially appropriate for leaders seeking to create an equipping environment in their congregation. "Down + Out: Where Grace Takes You" is a six-session DVD that explores the life to which God calls us. "Connecting Sunday to Monday" is a five-session DVD that stimulates discussion on the connection of faith and daily life. Marc Kolden's book, *The Christian's Calling in the World*, is a mere fifty pages, but will help stimulate conversation in small group settings. http://www. selectlearning.org/store

Intervarsity's **Graduate and Faculty Ministries** website offers helpful resources at http://gfm.intervarsity.org. Under the *Resources* tab, click on *Integration of Faith, Learning & Practice*. Intervarsity also offers a thorough bibliography for Christians in business at http://mba.intervarsity.org/resource/bibliography-christians-business.

The Academy of Management is the world's largest and oldest professional association for management scholars and organizational studies. They offer an interest group called **Management, Spirituality, and Religion** that focuses on interdisciplinary theoretical and applied research and pedagogy related to the relevance and relationship of spirituality and religion in management. http://group.aomonline.org/msr/

The **Institute for Faith, Work & Economics** is a Christian research organization committed to promoting biblical and economic principles that help individuals find fulfillment in their work and contribute to a free and flourishing society. http://tifwe.org

Patheos.com hosts an ongoing global dialogue about religion and spirituality. Under the *Channels* tab, choose *Topical Channels: Faith and Work*. http://www.patheos.com

Regent College in Vancouver, British Columbia, offers the **Marketplace Institute**. Their website says, "At the Marketplace Institute, we believe it is critical for Christians to learn from and be challenged by both culture and the church." The website offers ideas and resources to do that. http://marketplace.regent-college.edu

Luther Seminary (St. Paul, Minnesota) recently conducted the **Vibrant Congregations Initiative** to study how congregations develop vital, vibrant ministries in six critical areas, one of which is vocation. Visit http://www.luthersem.edu/vcp/default.aspx?m=6112. Click on *VCP Outcomes*, then choose *Vocation*.

The **London Institute for Contemporary Christianity** reports on some very encouraging work on making the connection between faith and work. *Supporting Christians at Work (without going crazy)* is a brief and practical guide designed to help churches and their leaders make the connection between faith and work. http://www.licc.org.uk

BOOKS

Work Matters: Connecting Sunday Worship to Monday Work (Nelson), is an accessible look at work through the lens of the Christian faith. The book provides helpful insights into the nature of work and helps Christians make the connection between faith and work. Nelson's accompanying website, http://workmattersbook.com, continues the conversation started in the book.

Work in the Spirit: Toward a Theology of Work (Volf), is a scholarly effort to develop a Protestant theology of work. Volf interprets work in terms of the doctrine of the Holy Spirit; in the process he rejects the understanding of work as vocation and adopts the concept of *charisma* as his theological foundation. He argues that all human work can be seen as cooperation with God in the care and transformation of the world.

There are a number of books that can supplement the material offered in Chapter 8, "**Rethinking Faith Formation**." To explore the shift from education to faith formation see *Traveling Together: A Guide for Disciple-Forming Congregations* (Jones); the chapter "The Way" in *From Nomads to Pilgrims* (Bass and Stewart-Sicking); Chapter 5, "Delivering the Goods (Part 2)" in *Transforming Congregational Culture* (Robinson); *Frogs without Legs Can't Hear* (Anderson and Hill); and *Cultivating Sent Communities: Missional Spiritual Formation* (Zscheile).

Bill Diehl's books remain classics in this field, even though they are now dated. ***Thank God It's Monday!*** is intended to help laity connect their Sunday faith to their Monday world. Diehl examines the ways in which modern "principalities and powers" control our lives and how the timeless message of the gospel gives us a sense of purpose and frees us from the captivity of culture.

Diehl's ***Monday Connection*** is helpful in two regards. On pages 52–55 he briefly describes a "Monday Connection" group that he started in his church. The group met monthly, at which a participant brought a real-life case study of a problem often (but not always) related to work. The group explored the problem with the presenter, but they would never tell the person what to do. The pastor was present as a biblical and theological resource person, but never as the "all-knowing authority on all subjects." They intentionally looked for connections between Sunday worship and the case study. In the rest of the book Diehl explores five ways in which we can incarnate ministry in daily life: the ministries of competency, presence, ethics, change, and values.

Related to Diehl's five types of ministry, see Miller's *God at Work*, especially chapters 4 and 7 for his "**Four E's**," four ways people seek to integrate faith and work: Ethics, Evangelism, Experience, and Enrichment.

Faith Goes to Work (Banks) provides a number of helpful essays. Janet Hagberg's chapter ("The Faith-Work Journey") describes stages of faith development and how that relates to faith at work. Chapters 3–10 provide first-person testimonials from people in a variety of professions who have worked to make a faith connection with their work.

Chapter 5 of ***Keeping Faith at Work*** (Krueger) describes five critical economic and workplace issues that Christians and others face in contemporary society. In the rest of the book he raises many questions, both in the "group discussion" section at the end of each chapter and throughout the book, that would be worthy focal points for small groups.

Resources to Feed Your Imagination

Chapter 7 of ***All God's People Are Ministers*** (Page) provides exercises, practical helps, and conversation starters that could easily be used in a congregation that wants to connect faith and life.

Chapter 3 of ***Ministry in Daily Life*** (Diehl) provides a long list of things that can be done in worship and throughout the congregation to affirm the callings of all God's people.

Resources continue to be created and discovered. See www.TheScattering.org for an updated list of resources.

Bibliography

Anderson, David and Paul Hill. *Frogs Without Legs Can't Hear: Nurturing Disciples in Home and Congregation*. Minneapolis: Augsburg Fortress, 2003.

Anderson, James D. and Ezra Earl Jones. *Ministry of the Laity*. San Francisco: Harper & Row, 1986.

Armstrong, Chris. "More from Tom Nelson at Redeeming Work." Patheos (June 17, 2014). http://www.patheos.com/blogs/missionwork/2014/06/more-from-tom-nelson-at-redeeming-work.

Bainton, Roland H. *Here I Stand: A Life of Martin Luther*. Nashville: Abingdon, 1950.

Bass, Diana Butler and Joseph Stewart-Sicking, eds. *From Nomads to Pilgrims: Stories from Practicing Congregations*. Herndon, VA: Alban Institute, 2006.

Bass, Diana Butler. *The Practicing Congregation: Imagining a New Old Church*. Herndon, VA: Alban Institute, 2004.

Bass, Dorothy C. and Susan Briehl, eds. *On Our Way: Christian Practices for Living a Whole Life*. Nashville: Upper Room, 2009.

Bass, Dorothy C., ed. *Practicing Our Faith: A Way of Life for Searching People*. San Francisco: Jossey-Bass, 2010.

Benefiel, Margaret. *Soul at Work: Spiritual Leadership in Organizations*. New York: Seabury, 2005.

Bennethum, D. Michael. *Listen! God Is Calling!: Luther Speaks of Vocation, Faith, and Work*. Minneapolis: Augsburg Fortress, 2003.

The Book of Common Prayer. New York: Seabury, 1977.

Book of Order (2013–2015). Louisville, KY: Office of the General Assembly, Presbyterian Church (U.S.A.), 2013.

The Book of Resolutions of The United Methodist Church—2012. Nashville: The United Methodist Publishing House, 2012.

Bosch, David J. *Transforming Mission: Paradigm Shifts in Theology of Mission*. Maryknoll, NY: Orbis, 1991.

Bouch, Richard. *The Faith-Work Window: Why Work Matters to Christianity in a Fallen World*. Enumclaw, WA: Pleasant Word, 2009.

Broholm, Dick, and John Hoffman. "Empowering Laity for Their Full Ministry." An unpublished and photocopied workbook that was part of the Andover Newton Laity Project, 1981.

Buchanan, John M. "Being Christ's Body." *The Christian Century*, March 5, 2014.

Calvin, John. *Institutes of the Christian Religion*. Philadelphia: Westminster, 1936.

Catechism of the Catholic Church. http://www.usccb.org/beliefs-and-teachings/what-we-believe/catechism/catechism-of-the-catholic-church/epub/index.cfm.

Cox, Harvey. *The Future of Faith.* New York: HarperOne, 2009.

Crabtree, Davida Foy. *The Empowering Church.* Herndon, VA: Alban Institute, 1989.

Daniel, Lillian. *Tell It Like It Is: Reclaiming the Practice of Testimony.* Herndon, VA: Alban Institute, 2006.

Diehl, William E. *Christianity and Real Life.* Philadelphia: Fortress, 1976.

———. *Ministry in Daily Life: A Practical Guide for Congregations.* Herndon, VA: Alban Institute, 1996.

———. *The Monday Connection: A Spirituality of Competence, Affirmation, and Support in the Workplace.* New York: HarperCollins, 1991.

———. *Thank God It's Monday!* Philadelphia: Fortress, 1982.

DuBois, Dwight L. "Your Minister at Walgreens." Alban Institute's *Congregations* magazine, 2012, Volume 1, Number 1, Issue 1.

Evangelical Lutheran Worship. Minneapolis: Augsburg Fortress, 2006.

Evanston Speaks. London: SCM Press, 1954.

Everist, Norma Cook, and Nelvin Vos. *Where in the World Are You? Connecting Faith and Daily Life.* Herndon, VA: Alban Institute, 1996.

Foss, Mike. *Power Surge: Six Marks of Discipleship for a Changing Church.* Minneapolis: Fortress, 2000

Frambach, Nathan, and Cheryl M. Peterson. "Church of the future," *The Lutheran*, March 2014.

Fry, Louis W., and Yochanan Altman. *Spiritual Leadership in Action.* Charlotte, NC: Information Age, 2013.

Fryer, Kelly A. *Reclaiming the "C" Word: Daring to be Church Again.* Minneapolis: Augsburg Fortress, 2006.

Gallup, George, Jr., and D. Michael Lindsay, *Surveying the Religious Landscape: Trends in U.S. Beliefs.* Harrisburg, PA: Morehouse, 1999.

Greene, Mark. *Supporting Christians at Work (without going crazy)* London: Administry, 2001.

Guder, Darrell L. *The Continuing Conversion of the Church.* Grand Rapids: William B. Eerdmans, 2000.

———, ed., *Missional Church: A Vision for the Sending of the Church in North America.* Grand Rapids: William B. Eerdmans, 1998.

Hall, Douglas John. *The Cross in Our Context: Jesus and the Suffering World.* Minneapolis: Fortress, 2003

Hunsberger, George R., and Craig Van Gelder. *The Church Between Gospel and Culture.* Grand Rapids: William B. Eerdmans, 1996.

Jacobs, Ryan. "Are Sundays Dying?" *Pacific Standard* (May 8, 2014). http://www.psmag.com/navigation/books-and-culture/sundays-terrible-weekends-dying-80943/.

Jones, Jeffrey D. *Traveling Together: A Guide for Disciple-Forming Congregations.* Herndon, VA: Alban Institute, 2006.

Jordan, Clarence. *The Substance of Faith and Other Cotton Patch Sermons.* Dallas Lee, ed. New York: Association Press, 1972.

Kolb, Robert, and Timothy J. Wengert, eds. *The Book of Concord: The Confessions of the Evangelical Lutheran Church.* Fortress: Minneapolis, 2000.

Kolden, Marc. *The Christian's Calling in the World.* St. Paul, MN: Centered Life, 2002.

BIBLIOGRAPHY

Kraemer, Hendrick. *A Theology of the Laity.* Vancouver, British Columbia: Regent College Publishing, 1958.

Krueger, David A. *Keeping Faith at Work: The Christian in the Workplace.* Nashville: Abingdon, 1994.

Long, Thomas G. *Testimony: Talking Ourselves into Being Christian.* San Francisco: Jossey-Bass, 2004.

Lose, David J. *Preaching at the Crossroads: How the World—and Our Preaching—Is Changing.* Minneapolis: Fortress, 2013.

Luther, Martin. *A Contemporary Translation of Luther's Small Catechism.* Minneapolis, Augsburg Fortress, 1996.

———. *Luther's Works.* Jaroslav Pelikan, Helmut T. Lehmann, and Christopher Boyd Brown, eds. 75 vols. Philadelphia: Fortress; St. Louis: Concordia Publishing House, 1955-.

———. *D. Martin Luthers Werke.* Kritische Gesamtausgabe (Weimarer Ausgabe). 73 vols. Weimar, 1883–2009.

Mallory, Sue. *The Equipping Church: Serving Together to Transform Lives.* Grand Rapids: Zondervan, 2001.

McHugh, Adam S. "Can introverts lead?" *The Christian Century* (November 17, 2009). http://www.christiancentury.org/article/2009–11/can-introverts-lead.

McNeal, Reggie. *Missional Renaissance: Changing the Scorecard for the Church.* San Francisco: Jossey-Bass, 2009.

McWilliams Dickhart, Judith. *Church-going Insider or Gospel-carrying Outsider: A different view of congregations.* Division for Ministry: Evangelical Lutheran Church in America, 2002.

Miller, David W. *God at Work: The History and Promise of the Faith at Work Movement.* New York: Oxford University Press, 2007.

Mouw, Richard J. *Called to Holy Worldliness.* Philadelphia: Fortress, 1980.

Nelson, Tom. "A Pastoral Prayer." Christ Community Church (May 19, 2014). http://www.ccefc.org/_blog/Featured_News_and_Events/post/a-pastoral-prayer/#sthash.scfb4h4d.dpuf.

———. *Work Matters: Connecting Sunday Worship to Monday Work.* Wheaton, IL: Crossway, 2011.

Nessan, Craig L. *Beyond Maintenance to Mission: A Theology of the Congregation.* 2nd ed. Minneapolis: Fortress, 2010.

———. *Shalom Church: The Body of Christ as Ministering Community.* Minneapolis: Fortress, 2010.

Ogden, Greg. *Unfinished Business: Returning Ministry to the People of God.* Grand Rapids: Zondervan, 2003.

Olsen, Charles M. *Transforming Church Boards into Communities of Spiritual Leaders.* Herndon, VA: Alban Institute, 1995.

Page, Patricia. *All God's People Are Ministers: Equipping Church Members for Ministry.* Minneapolis: Augsburg Fortress, 1993.

Peck, George, and John S. Hoffman, eds. *The Laity in Ministry: The Whole People of God for the Whole World.* Valley Forge, PA: Judson, 1984.

Prentiss, Demi and Fletcher Lowe. *Radical Sending: Go to Love and Serve.* New York: Morehouse, 2015.

Reese, Martha Grace. *Unbinding the Gospel: Real Life Evangelism.* St. Louis: Chalice, 2008.

Robinson, Anthony B. *Transforming Congregational Culture*. Grand Rapids: William B. Eerdmans, 2003.

Roxburgh, Alan, and Fred Romanuk. *The Missional Leader: Equipping Your Church to Reach a Changing World*. San Francisco: Jossey-Bass, 2006.

Scharen, Christian. *Faith as a Way of Life: A Vision for Pastoral Leadership*. Grand Rapids: William B. Eerdmans, 2008.

Schuurman, Douglas J. *Vocation: Discerning Our Callings in Life*. Grand Rapids: William B. Eerdmans, 2004.

Schweizer, R. Eduard. "Ministry in the Early Church," *The Anchor Bible Dictionary* (vol. 4). New York: Doubleday, 1992.

Simpson, J. A. and E. S. C. Weiner. *The Oxford English Dictionary*. Oxford: Clarendon Press, 1989.

Stevens, R. Paul, and Phil Collins. *The Equipping Pastor: A Systems Approach to Congregational Leadership*. Herndon VA: Alban Institute, 1993.

Stevens, R. Paul. *Liberating the Laity: Equipping All the Saints for Ministry*. Downers Grove, IL: Intervarsity, 1985.

———. *The Other Six Days: Vocation, Work, and Ministry in Biblical Perspective*. Vancouver, British Columbia: Regent College Publishing, 1999.

Swanson, Roger K., and Shirley F. Clement. *The Faith-Sharing Congregation*. Nashville: Discipleship Resources, 2003.

Trueblood, Elton. *The Incendiary Fellowship*. New York: Harper and Row, 1967.

The United Methodist Hymnal. Nashville: The United Methodist Publishing House, 1989.

Van Gelder, Craig. *The Essence of the Church: A Community Created by the Spirit*. Grand Rapids: Baker, 2000.

Veith, Gene Edward Jr. *God at Work: Your Christian Vocation in All of Life*. Wheaton, IL: Crossway, 2002.

Volf, Miroslav. *Work in the Spirit: Toward a Theology of Work*. Eugene, OR: Wipf and Stock, 2001.

White, Edward A. "The Sunday-Monday Gap: Resistances in Church and World to Connecting Faith and Work." In *Faith Goes to Work: Reflections from the Marketplace*, edited by Robert J. Banks. Eugene, OR: Wipf and Stock, 1999.

Wingren, Gustaf. *Luther on Vocation*. Eugene, OR: Wipf and Stock, 2004.

Zscheile, Dwight J., ed. *Cultivating Sent Communities: Missional Spiritual Formation*. Grand Rapids: William B. Eerdmans, 2012.

Index of Subjects

Abraham, covenant with, 3
active member, 26, 45, 95, 98, 99, 102, 147
Affirmation of Baptism liturgy, Lutheran, 39
Affirmation of Christian Vocation, Lutheran, 133n10
affirming scattered ministries, 102, 125
Anderson-Larson, Virginia, 143n21
anticlericalism, 83–85
apostles, 35, 59, 111
Apostolic Fathers, 63
autoimmune disorder, x–x1, 78–81, 83, 88

Bainton, Roland, 72
Bass, Diana Butler, 135
Bass and Briehl, 135n13
Belgic Confession, 8
Benefiel, Margaret, 78n19
Bennethum, Michael, 71n2
bishop (overseer), 59–60, 63–64
Bonhoeffer, Dietrich, xi, 18n38
Book of Concord, 7n7
Bosch, David, 8n9, 9n12, 63n21, 64–65
Broholm and Hoffman, 67n30, 84n4
Buchanan, John, 146
bungee jumping, 12–15
busyness, 27, 37–38, 43, 93–95, 129

Calvin, John, 8, 72
Catechism of the Catholic Church, 8–9
"checking in" experiment, 127
Christian freedom, x–xi

church: as "the people," 17, 20; as "sign and foretaste, agent and instrument," 18, 89; definition of, 7–9, 16–17, 20, 71; nature and purpose, 1–5, 30; uses of, 1
church-centered church, 97–100
"The church of christ, in every age," xi
clergy and laity, distinction, 65–68, 88–91
clergy in the New Testament, 50–63
clericalism, ix, 84–85
competition between church and life, xv, 41, 43, 94
concrete v. general references to ministry, 11, 41–43, 45–46, 113, 117, 125–26, 128, 131–32
Constantine, Emperor, 64
Council of Trent, 8
counterintuitive nature of the scattered church, 92, 95, 146
Cox, Harvey, 5, 64n23
Crabtree, Davida Foy, 20n41, 26, 112, 114, 118–20
culture and systems, 103, 119–21, 139

daily bread, 47–48, 74–75
Daniel, Lillian, 130–31
diaconal ministry, xi, 88, 142
diakonia/os, 53, 57, 59, 63, 65, 67, 89
Diehl, William, 26, 79–80, 133n11, 152
dream of God, 5–7, 13, 18, 89, 95, 99, 103, 119, 135
dying to ourselves, 93–96, 103–4

Einstein, Albert, ix, xi–xii

Index of Scripture References

INDEX OF SCRIPTURE REFERENCES